SANDSABLAZE

· GRAND PRIX GREATNESS ·
from HARRISBURG to the OLYMPICS

*All the best,
Kim Gatto*

KIMBERLY GATTO

with BUDDY BROWN
foreword by GEORGE H. MORRIS

Charleston — London

THE
History
PRESS

Published by The History Press
Charleston, SC 29403
www.historypress.net

First published 2014

Manufactured in the United States

ISBN 978.1.62619.530.1

Library of Congress CIP data applied for.

Inside his chest beats the heart of a lion.
—Greek proverb

This book is dedicated in memory of "Pappy,"
the little horse with the heart of a lion.

CONTENTS

Contents

FOREWORD

K imberly Gatto has written a fascinating and most factual account of Buddy Brown and his legendary Sandsablaze. Not only is this a unique story of a great horse and a great rider, but it is also a most interesting and historical cross-reference for those interested in equestrian sport.

My teacher-student relationship with Buddy began decades before we first met. Most, if not all, of the key players in Buddy and Sandsablaze's story were friends of mine. Anne Parry Weser and I were the best of friends at the New Canaan Country Day School in the early 1940s. Her mother and my mother were also the best of friends, as her mother was Ginnie Moss's best friend from the Deep South (Georgia). "Pappy," the nickname of Ginnie Moss's husband, was always Sandsablaze's barn name.

Meredith McLaughlin (we called her "Mugs" growing up—I still do!) grew up riding at the Fairfield County Hunt Club under Emerson Burr in the 1950s. I rode at the Ox Ridge Hunt Club in Darien, Connecticut. But every day around noon, after working my horse in the summer, I would head up the Post Road or the Merritt Parkway to Fairfield. They had all the prettiest girls. Pamela Turnure (later on President Kennedy's staff) and Ronnie la Roche (Rosalind Russell's niece) were just two of the many.

Joey Darby first started with Linky Smith, a well-known jumper rider, in Maryland. Later in the 1970s, Joey and I were fierce competitors in the working hunter division—he with Balalaika and myself on Isle of Erin.

Sandsablaze and San Man, both started by Mugs McLaughlin, ended up with me at Hunterdon in the early 1970s. I do not think I knew until years later of their similar breeding and identical starts. Both horses had brilliant, though different, careers at the top of the sport.

I got to know Bob Freels and his future wife, Jeri, around 1957, when I started working with Bert de Némethy and the United States Equestrian Team. Bob was a top-class horseman from Tennessee and ran a tight ship for Bert. We were all part of Bert's first real team and went to Europe together (1958, 1959 and 1960).

Pattie and Graham Brown initially lived in Darien, Connecticut, and started riding at Ox Ridge. I turned professional and would teach at Ox Ridge on Tuesday nights. I got to know the Browns socially at Ox Ridge but never taught them. At that time, Graham rode with my mentor, Victor Hugo-Vidal Jr. Tania Forman (now Tania Nagro), one of my best and oldest friends and students, sold Graham one of his early horses through Artie Hawkins, another old friend.

Of course, I was aware of Buddy from the beginning on the ponies. Buddy, like Katie Monahan, Conrad Homfeld and Leslie Burr, was a child prodigy. Right from the get-go, he had an incredible "touch" and empathy for a horse. Then, with his horse Sourball, Buddy became a force to be reckoned with in the junior hunter division under Bob Freels's tutelage.

At some point, Bob Freels and/or Graham Brown called me to meet and talk about Buddy. They thought I was the right one to get Buddy started in the jumpers. Of course, I was thrilled and honored at the prospect of having this particular young rider as a pupil. At our first meeting, I made it clear that I wanted Buddy to have the discipline of the hunter seat equitation division as he was learning the jumpers. I had seen Sandsablaze and thought he could do the job.

Let me be honest—Sandsablaze, as great a horse as he turned out to be in the jumper ring, was not a great hunter. He was attractive but not pretty, a less-than-average mover and did not have the perfect jumping style of a hunter. I saw the horse's future as a junior jumper/equitation horse—no more. Never, ever, in the beginning did I foresee that horse being an international horse, let alone an Olympic horse. Sandsablaze obviously appeared to have limited scope.

Buddy began to ride with me over the winter of 1971–72. I had just bought the property in Pittstown, New Jersey, which I called Hunterdon after the county, and did not put up an indoor ring for several years. When Buddy rode with me, we only rode outside, often without stirrups, and jumped all natural fences. I was physically, mentally and emotionally tough on Buddy. It was what he needed in order to harden him for his future in the jumper ring.

Buddy could not join us that winter in Florida. He stayed home to show locally and start to qualify for the Medal and the Maclay, as well as do some schooling jumper classes. One night, my old friend Michael Page called after the Old Salem show to tell me how impressed he was with Buddy and Sandsablaze jumping big fences. I was irritated he was jumping too big but elated at the same time.

I owned a wonderful older Thoroughbred open jumper named Big Line. I showed him myself from 1963 to 1964 and then passed him on to my top student at the time. Big Line really started the following four boys in the jumper division: Jimmy Kohn, Conrad Homfeld, James Hulick and Buddy Brown. Quite an accomplishment for one horse!

At Devon at the end of May, between the rain, the mud, the wide oxers and the warm-up fences I built, Buddy was on the ground four times. I look back on it as a positive, toughening-up experience for Buddy. In any case, it got him ready for the upcoming European experience.

Buddy Brown won the AHSA Medal Finals in 1973. That's a pretty good accomplishment for any horse and any rider. He and Sandsablaze were equitation stars as well as jumper stars. Buddy always retained—and he still does to this day—his incredible touch on a hunter. My goal with all my "A-list" young riders was to work with Bert de Némethy and the USET. Buddy "won" the screening trials under Bert in 1973. Bert loved Buddy and, of course, was a good friend of mine as well as Bob and Jeri Freels. After Buddy's Medal win, it was time for Bert to start orchestrating Buddy's career.

Buddy was still with me in 1974. Of course, he was almost a "shoe-in" to win the Maclay finals at Madison Square Garden. However, we had to make a choice between riding on the team or going for the Maclay. Buddy and I talked about it for a split second. Our decisions were the same: ride on the team!

I can remember it like it was yesterday. Buddy and Graham brought another green Thoroughbred down to Hunterdon for lessons. He was a big, attractive grey called "A Little Bit." I ran to the phone, called Bert and said, "He's got another one!" And sure enough, the horse turned out to be another international jumper. Buddy, Graham and Bob could find good horses under rocks!

In 1976, we were at the Montreal Olympic Games. The individual competition was held in Bromont on sand, all-weather footing, and the fences in the two-round competition were enormous. It rained and rained in Canada that year. The Nations Cup team competition traditionally was held in those days as the last event in the main Olympic track and field stadium. It obviously had to be the last event because the horses tore up the turf. Not having accreditation at that time, I was sitting in the spectator seating just above the arena. Buddy walked the Nations Cup course and then approached me. His words were: "George, this course is ridiculous. It's like a four-foot-six junior jumper course!" Because of the nonstop rain and the shallow non-horsey turf, the footing was treacherous. The horses could hardly stand up, and I'd say the French won by default. Since Montreal, Seoul (1988 Olympic Games) was the only Games to take the Nations Cup to the main stadium. Now all equestrian events are held at a horse-friendly venue.

Later in the 1970s, at the Branchville show, I was standing at the in-gate watching the jump-off of the grand prix. Buddy and Sandsablaze jumped the last fence coming right toward the in-gate and won the class; then the horse broke his leg coming through the timers. It was an unbelievable and heartbreaking moment—like when Trail Guide died at Madison Square Garden or when Hickstead died in the ring in Italy.

Buddy Brown and Sandsablaze (Pappy) were a storybook, legendary pair. They showed us what a partnership can bring. And the big lesson is that you can never tell about a horse. Horses always surprise us, and Sandsablaze certainly did. Here was a horse that shouldn't, couldn't, wouldn't—but did.

George H. Morris
Wellington, Florida
May 26, 2014

ACKNOWLEDGEMENTS

This book has been in process for more than a year. It would not have been possible without the efforts of many who have helped along the way.

First and foremost, I am grateful to Buddy Brown, who entrusted me to share the story of his amazing equine partner and friend. Buddy spent countless hours recounting his memories of his time spent with "Pappy," reviewing the manuscript as it was written and contributing photographs from his personal collection. Without Buddy's contribution and his dedication to Pappy, this work would not have been possible.

Buddy's father, Graham Brown, also spent innumerable hours sharing memories of his family and of Pappy and carefully reviewed the manuscript on numerous occasions for accuracy. I am grateful to Graham and am honored to be a part of his family's story.

Vanessa Brown, Buddy's wife, first put me in touch with Buddy and offered valuable support along the way.

Jimmy Herring, Robert Ridland, Michael Matz, Sally Walker, Meredith McLaughlin, Joey Darby, Robin Rost Fairclough and Bill Rube took time out of their busy schedules to share their memories of Pappy with me and reviewed parts of the manuscript for accuracy, with additional thanks to Sally, Joey and Meredith for sending me photographs from their personal collections.

Dani McGrath, Beth Rowland and Joy Dunn provided support and friendship from the inception of this project, as well as timely and insightful answers to my many questions along the way.

ACKNOWLEDGEMENTS

Molly Sorge at the *Chronicle of the Horse* provided me with photographs and other information from the *Chronicle*'s archives.

Karl Leck, Senan Healey of the RDS Archives, Maureen Pethick of the USET Foundation, Pam Williams of the Belair Stable Museum and Cathy Schenck of the Keeneland Library provided me with wonderful photographs to include in the book.

My veterinarian, Dr. Jeremy Murdock, shared his memories of Dublin and the atmosphere at the Grand Prix.

Allison Pareis and Patrick Lennon performed thorough reviews of the manuscript and provided valuable support and friendship along the way.

Louise Ferro Martin, Monika Herrington, Anita Leary, Margaret Schubert, Michael Blowen, Beth Harris, Jennie Carleton, Frank Waters and Gretchen Albertini reviewed portions of the manuscript and/or provided information, assistance and friendship during the writing process.

My commissioning editor, Whitney Landis of The History Press, believed in the project from the beginning, and project editor Will Collicott provided excellent support and feedback.

All of my friends and family members have provided unending support, particularly my mom, Ann Gatto Urquhart, who has always believed in me as a writer, horsewoman, daughter and friend.

K.A.G.

PREFACE

The immortal Shakespeare once penned the words, "The most splendid gift of all is a noble horse." Centuries after that line was written, it still rings correct. A true horseman views every equine as a gift, each with its own set of examples and teachings. If one is lucky, he may be blessed with a "horse of a lifetime"—a special animal with whom he forges an undeniable, lasting bond. This horse might not be the greatest athlete or the most elegant, but when paired with the right rider, it can achieve what was once deemed impossible.

In the grueling sport of show jumping, the legendary Sandsablaze was an unlikely hero. Standing barely sixteen hands, the lanky, ewe-necked gelding hardly looked the part of an elite champion. In his early years, the horse's legs seemed too long for his body, and he often jumped unevenly, showing little indication of future glory. As many believed that he lacked the scope to tackle a junior jumper course, the huge fences of the grand prix ring were barely a consideration. Then there was the question of speed and agility. While show jumpers tackle quick, twisting turns with ease, Sandsablaze could often be clumsy and lethargic. Still, what the little horse seemingly lacked in natural scope, he more than made up for in sheer heart.

Sandsablaze's great heart propelled him, along with his young owner/ rider, William "Buddy" Brown, over the most daunting of obstacles and into history as one of the great icons of the sport. True to his name, which was derived from the *Arabian Nights* folk tales, Sandsablaze became Brown's own "magic carpet ride," carrying the young rider into a world of international

In a partnership spanning more than eight years, Buddy Brown and Sandsablaze shared a strong bond. *Photo by Karl Leck.*

stardom. The two developed a partnership based on mutual respect and trust. Brown put his faith in the leggy Thoroughbred, and Sandsablaze gave his all to please his master.

The pair's early days were far from easy; there were many falls and disappointments along the way. But as the bond strengthened between young Brown and Sandsablaze, there was seemingly nothing beyond their reach. Following their win at the AHSA Medal Finals—the ultimate triumph for a junior rider—the pair achieved what had thus far been deemed impossible: graduating to the grand prix ranks. Their record-setting victory in the Grand Prix of Ireland, when Brown was only eighteen years old, has yet to be duplicated.

Buddy Brown and Sandsablaze would go on to win several international events—including team gold medals at two different Pan Am Games—and represented the United States at the Olympics, the pinnacle of competition for any athlete. To the surprise of the crowds at Toronto's Royal Winter Fair, Brown and the little Thoroughbred cleared a monstrous seven-foot-one-inch wall, a lofty accomplishment even for a much larger horse. Years later, in his final moments, Pappy would once again give his heart to Brown, thrilling the crowds with one last victory before suffering what proved to be a fatal injury.

Not all horsemen are gifted with a noble steed. But for those of us who are lucky enough to spend a lifetime with horses, there is always the possibility of being blessed with such an animal. In a partnership with Brown that spanned more than eight years, the little Thoroughbred more than proved himself worthy of Shakespeare's words. With his massive heart and undeniable spirit, Sandsablaze was indeed the most splendid of gifts—not only to Buddy Brown, but also to the world at large.

CHAPTER 1

IN THE BEGINNING

D ecades before Sandsablaze cleared his first fence, his ancestors were galloping to victory on America's most prestigious racetracks. In fact, had the little Thoroughbred's life taken a more standard course, it is likely that he would have begun his career as his ancestors had—on the track. Sandsablaze was descended on his sire's side from two equine legends of the turf; his great-grandsire, Reigh Count, won the Kentucky Derby, and his grandsire, Count Fleet, captured the now-elusive Triple Crown. Both horses were owned by John D. Hertz, founder of the Yellow Cab Company, which later became the car rental corporation that now bears his name.

Hertz, a colorful character with wire-rimmed spectacles and slicked-back hair, knew a good horse when he saw one. The European-born businessman, who made a fortune in the transport business, liked to brag to friends that he "knew how to pick 'em." On a summer day in 1927 at bucolic Saratoga Race Course, Hertz proved that to be the case.

Hertz was watching the morning races when a lanky chestnut caught his eye. The colt, known as Reigh Count, was not the most talented of the lot; rather, another quality had drawn Hertz's attention. While galloping in company toward the finish, Reigh Count reached over and bit an opponent squarely on the neck. Hertz, a former prizefighter who had boxed under the name Dan Donnelly, was thoroughly impressed with the fractious animal. "I've always admired a fighter," Hertz allegedly said at the time. "Man or horse."[1]

While Hertz appreciated Reigh Count's fiery disposition, the horse's owner, Willis Sharp Kilmer, was less than impressed. Kilmer boasted a string of great champions in his barn, including the legendary gelding Exterminator, winner of the 1918 Kentucky Derby. Kilmer had neither the affection nor the patience for a horse that was not earning his keep, and in seven starts, the volatile Reigh Count had yet to win a single race. Therefore, when Hertz made an offer of $10,000 for the colt, Kilmer accepted readily, notwithstanding the objections of his trainer, Henry McDaniel.

McDaniel recognized Reigh Count's innate talent, noting that the horse was simply slow to mature. As such, he pleaded with Kilmer to hang on to the colt a bit longer, but the stubborn owner refused to reconsider. A deal was finalized, and Reigh Count joined the stable of John Hertz and his wife, Fannie. The couple boasted several horse farms to their name, including Stoner Creek Farm in Paris, Kentucky, located just outside Lexington.

Within months, it became clear that Hertz's instincts had indeed been correct. Racing under the vibrant taxi-yellow silks of the Hertz stable, Reigh Count matured into a poised competitor. By the end of that season, he was widely regarded as one of the top colts of his class. Reigh Count soared to victory in two key races—the Walden Handicap and the Kentucky Jockey Club Stakes—and lost only one start thereafter, which many attributed to an error by his jockey. In that race, the Belmont Futurity, Reigh Count was beaten by a whisker at the wire by his stablemate Anita Peabody. So close was the finish that the *New York Times* posted a photograph in which the two jockeys, side by side at the wire, stared at each other in disbelief.

Reigh Count bounced back from this questionable defeat to dominate in his three-year-old season. He romped in the Kentucky Derby at Churchill Downs, bringing home the coveted garland of roses and earning a place in racing lore. Regrettably, Reigh Count sustained an injury following the race and was sidelined from both the Preakness and the Belmont Stakes, the remaining jewels in the Triple Crown of American racing.

Reigh Count returned to form later that summer at Belmont Park, where he handily defeated Victorian, winner of that year's Preakness, in the Lawrence Realization Stakes. He capped off the season with a win over older horses in Belmont's Jockey Club Gold Cup over an exhausting two miles on the dirt. While no formal "horse of the year" award was presented at that time, Reigh Count was widely recognized by the media as the best colt of 1928. The following season, the horse was shipped to England, where he won the coveted Coronation Cup in an exciting finish at the wire.

Following this victory overseas, *Time* magazine reported that owner John Hertz had refused an offer of $1 million for Reigh Count. Hertz quipped to the media, "I think a fellow who would pay $1 million for a horse ought

Kentucky Derby winner Reigh Count was the great-grandsire of Sandsablaze. *Photo courtesy of Keeneland/Cook.*

to have his head examined, and the fellow who turned it down must be absolutely unbalanced."[2] Had this offer been accepted, it would have been the largest amount ever paid for a racehorse at that time.

Reigh Count was retired to stud at Hertz's Kentucky farm, where, in the years that followed, he would sire twenty-two graded stakes winners. In 1937, as Reigh Count was gaining in years, John Hertz purchased a brown sprint mare called Quickly in an effort to expand his breeding program. The mare, a winner of thirty-two races, carried the bloodlines of the stallion The Tetrarch, who was hailed as one of the greatest two-year-olds ever to race in England.

Quickly was sent to Reigh Count in the spring of 1939, and on the morning of March 24, 1940, the mare delivered the offspring of this mating. The lanky, brown colt with spindly legs appeared to have inherited his sire's fiery disposition. The new foal was given the name Count Fleet, with the "Count" lifted from the name of his sire and "Fleet" added in homage to Hertz's line of business. From his earliest days, Count Fleet proved difficult to handle, biting and striking the stable workers. While Hertz had admired the "fighting spirit" shown by Reigh Count on the track, he quickly developed a disdain for the young and rambunctious foal. Soon Hertz decided to offer Count Fleet for sale.

The colt was not an easy sell, as would-be buyers were unimpressed with his extra-long legs and seemingly frail build. Count Fleet's lack of manners was another point of contention; his misbehavior discouraged more than one potential buyer. As Hertz lamented his failure to sell the gangly colt, stable employee Sam Ramsen noted that the horse was showing promise. "Someday he's going to be one fine racer," Ramsen allegedly told Hertz. "When that leggy brown colt wants to run, he can just about fly."[3]

Ramsen's words proved to be correct when the colt began his career on the track. As a juvenile, Count Fleet was never out of the money in fifteen starts. That season, he smashed the Belmont Park track record for one mile and set a new world record in the Champagne Stakes. He subsequently won the Pimlico Futurity by five lengths over the favoured Occupation, equalling the track record in the process. Count Fleet then dominated the Walden Stakes at Pimlico by a whopping thirty lengths, en route to being named the year's best juvenile.

While he showed winning form on the racetrack, Count Fleet was often prone to dangerous vices such as bucking and rearing. This behavior did not sit well with owner John Hertz, who feared that the horse would injure or perhaps kill jockey Johnny Longden. As America was in the midst of a war and Hertz was downsizing his string of racers, he attempted, once again, to sell Count Fleet. Longden, however, was opposed to the sale; despite the horse's poor manners, he felt a strong affinity for the animal. When Longden found out that a buyer was about to make an offer on Count Fleet, the jockey bicycled frantically to the nearest phone booth to telephone Hertz and stop the sale. After much pleading on the part of the jockey, Hertz agreed to keep the colt.

Longden continued to work with the horse, and by the dawn of his three-year-old season, Count Fleet had become the talk of the sport. In the Wood Memorial at New York's old Jamaica racetrack, Count Fleet easily defeated the highly touted Blue Swords, solidifying his position as the favorite for the Kentucky Derby. After sustaining an injury to his left hind leg, however, there was question as to whether Count Fleet would be able to compete at Churchill Downs on the first Saturday in May. Once again, jockey Longden intervened. He convinced Hertz to transport the horse by rail to Louisville, where they would further evaluate his soundness. According to sources, for the duration of the journey, Longden stood holding an ice pack against the horse's injured leg.

Longden's tending to the injury was successful, and Count Fleet was back to winning form on Derby Day. The colt handily defeated his opponents by three lengths at Churchill Downs, duplicating the victory of his sire and earning a second Derby cup for John and Fannie Hertz. A mere week later, Count Fleet returned to winning form in the Preakness, where he blasted the field by eight lengths over a muddy track at Pimlico Race Course. In between the Preakness and the Belmont, he added the Withers Stakes to his growing list of victories, dominating the field by a full five lengths.

By the time of the running of the third jewel in the Triple Crown, only two horses showed up to face the reigning Derby and Preakness champ at Belmont Park. Count Fleet put on a show for the masses, soaring to victory by a whopping twenty-five lengths and finishing two-fifths of a second ahead of the existing track record.

Triple Crown winner Count Fleet, grandsire of Sandsablaze, is shown here in later years at Stoner Creek Farm. *Photo courtesy of Keeneland/Meadors.*

After the Belmont trophy was presented and the horse was led back into the stable, grooms noticed an injury to Count Fleet's right front ankle. It appeared as if the horse had clipped himself during the race, but his handlers felt confident that the wound was merely superficial. Regrettably, the injury did not respond well to treatment, and Count Fleet was forced into early retirement. His brilliance that season, however, earned him unanimous selection as both champion three-year-old male and horse of the year. Count Fleet's record of sixteen wins in twenty-one starts, with earnings of $250,300, would later earn him induction into the National Museum of Racing Hall of Fame. In the decades to come, Count Fleet's name would appear in the pedigrees of many successful hunters and jumpers.

CHAPTER 2
BIRTH OF A LEGEND

After winning the coveted Triple Crown, Count Fleet retired in a blaze of glory and promptly began stud duty at the Hertzes' Stoner Creek Farm. He was widely regarded as one of the premier stallions of the era, topping the American list as the leading sire in 1951. Count Fleet produced a total of 39 stakes winners, including Kentucky Derby champion Count Turf and two winners of the Belmont Stakes. Additionally, he was the maternal grandsire of 118 stakes winners, the most famous of which was Kelso, five-time horse of the year. Like many of Count Fleet's descendants, Kelso showed a penchant for jumping; the gelding spent his post-racing years as a foxhunter for owner Allaire DuPont.

Blazing Count was one of Count Fleet's lesser-known progeny. Foaled in 1952, the lanky dappled grey failed to match the success of his sire on the track, although he did finish in the money in fourteen of twenty-three starts. The colt's most notable finish was a second place in the 1955 Belmont Stakes over a gruelling one-and-a-half mile distance. In that race, Blazing Count was bested by Belair Stud's legendary Nashua, who would later be named horse of the year. Blazing Count earned a total of $42,100 on the track before being retired to stallion duty in 1956; his first crop of foals would arrive the following year.

In the spring of 1966, Blazing Count was mated with a chestnut mare called Sandy Atlas at the request of the mare's owner, William Manis. While the details of Sandy Atlas's life are far removed from the annals of history, one quality—heart—shines through the pages of her racing records. The

Blazing Count, sire of Sandsablaze, was a son of Triple Crown winner Count Fleet. *Photo by E.H. Spratlin, courtesy of Keeneland/Thoroughbred Times.*

Blazing Count (left) placed second behind Belair Stud's noted champion, Nashua, in the 1955 Belmont Stakes. *Photo courtesy of the Belair Stable Museum.*

mare completed 125 starts in an eight-year-period, an exhausting amount by any standard. She posted 18 career wins, with total earnings of $18,900, and finished in the money in 37 races.

Sandy Atlas's heart and courage may have, in fact, been bred into in the mare's bloodlines. Her sire, Ladysman, was arguably the best juvenile of 1932, winning seven out of his nine starts that year and placing second in the remaining two. Among his victories were the top races open to two-year-olds: the Hopeful Stakes and the Grand Union Hotel Stakes, both held at historic Saratoga Race Course. Sandy Atlas's dam, Lotus Flower, also boasted noble bloodlines; her sire was the multiple stakes winner Whichone, the primary rival of U.S. Triple Crown champion Gallant Fox.

Retired to broodmare duty at the age of ten, Sandy Atlas would produce three fillies before ultimately delivering two chestnut colts. While all three fillies would embark on race careers, only one appeared to have inherited her dam's great heart. That filly, Sissy San, made 101 starts over a nine-year career, including a placing in stakes company in the 1963 Belleville Handicap. Following the birth of Sissy San, Sandy Atlas endured several

Ladysman was the sire of Sandsablaze's dam, Sandy Atlas. *Photo courtesy of Keeneland/Cook.*

unsuccessful seasons as a broodmare before producing a colt by Landman on February 24, 1966. In the months following the delivery of this foal, to be registered by the name of San Man, Sandy Atlas was bred to Blazing Count.

In the dark, early morning hours of April 17, 1967, Sandy Atlas delivered her Blazing Count foal—a bright chestnut colt with ivory markings. Like all American-born Thoroughbreds, the new foal was registered with The Jockey Club and, as was often the case, given a name that combined those of his sire and his dam. The name chosen for this new colt was Sandsablaze, a near-perfect unification of the names Sandy Atlas and Blazing Count.

The name Sandsablaze has an interesting history, having first appeared in the *Arabian Nights*, a series of popular folk tales dating back to the 1700s. These books, which originated in Persia, introduced the world to classic stories such as "Aladdin and the Magic Lamp" and "Ali Baba and the Forty Thieves." Also included within these pages, along with genies and magic carpets, was the character of Sandsablaze, a proud, golden stallion with a white face and four stockings. In these books, the fictional Sandsablaze was described as being "destined for great things to come."

Like the mythological character of the *Arabian Nights*, the new foal Sandsablaze had markings that matched the work of an artist's brush. The colt had what modern horsemen would describe as "a lot of chrome"—a white blaze and four tall, snow-white stockings. One—the front left—extended well above the knee, while the other foreleg bore a splash of white that resembled an upside-down "V." His hind legs mirrored the patterns of the front, with one white stocking extending nearly to his hock. With these markings and a small bit of white under his belly, Sandsablaze had what one photographer described as a "great paint job."

Very little detail is known about Sandsablaze's earliest days and months. As is the course with all foals, he likely stood up shortly after birth and spent his first few months alongside his mother. It is known that his breeder was a kindly gentleman who provided the utmost care to his animals. Sandsablaze was therefore treated gently and with respect, which likely factored in the development of his willing disposition. Like the character in *Arabian Nights* whose name he now carried, the little chestnut horse was indeed "destined for great things to come."

CHAPTER 3
TWO TRIPS TO KEENELAND

Nestled within the sprawling bluegrass of Lexington, Kentucky, Keeneland Race Course is a horseman's paradise. It is a place of emerald beauty where pin oaks, sycamores and maple trees line the paddocks to create an old-world charm. Established in 1935, Keeneland ranks among the most beautiful racetracks in the nation, an achievement that is topped only by its history. As host for the annual Blue Grass Stakes—one of the key prep races for the Kentucky Derby—Keeneland has launched the careers of many Thoroughbred legends.

While superstars like Northern Dancer and Spectacular Bid achieved pre-Derby wins on the Keeneland track, others got their start in its sales pavilion. The racecourse boasts the world's largest Thoroughbred auction house, with several sales held each year. This tradition originated in 1943, born out of necessity rather than fashion. During the war, restrictions were placed on travel by rail, the primary form of transport for horses from state to state. Southern breeders were unable to ship their young stock north to the sale at Saratoga Springs and thus convened to find a solution. The result was the establishment of Keeneland's first-ever Thoroughbred sale, which was held under a tent in the racetrack paddock.

That inaugural auction was an immediate success, earning itself a righteous place in racing history. One of the horses sold at Keeneland—a young Thoroughbred by the name of Hoop Jr.—would go on to win America's premier race, the Kentucky Derby, in 1945. The sale of Hoop Jr. effectively put Keeneland on the map as a venue for selling potential Derby champions. As the years rolled on, the sales grew in both size and prestige. Keeneland showcased the best young Thoroughbreds and attracted throngs of deep-pocketed buyers. These men and women searched, often in vain, for a glimpse of the next Kentucky Derby winner.

By 1969, the Keeneland sales had become large enough to warrant the establishment of a state-of-the-art pavilion, a necessary addition to accommodate the growing numbers of horses and would-be buyers. Around this time, when American Thoroughbreds dominated the hunter/jumper show rings, Keeneland's attraction expanded beyond the realm of horse racing. It became common practice for sport horse trainers—from hunters and jumpers to eventers and foxhunters—to travel to Keeneland in search of a young prospect. Thoroughbreds not acquired by race-minded buyers would often be purchased at Keeneland to find their niche on a fox hunt or in the show ring.

A 1969 photo of the Keeneland sales pavilion, where Sandsablaze was purchased by Meredith McLaughlin. *Photo courtesy of the Keeneland Association.*

Prior to the advent of the warmblood as a show horse, the Thoroughbred was preferred over other breeds, particularly when tackling an outside course peppered with aikens, coops and authentic brush boxes. Most Thoroughbreds were naturally sure-footed and scopey, and many possessed a strong work ethic. They relished the act of clearing fences over sometimes-uneven grassy terrain, and their flowing stride carried them stylishly from fence to fence. Their stamina and courage—often referred to as Thoroughbred "heart"—made them bold over fences that other breeds found intimidating. In the jumper ring, the speed that was inherent in the Thoroughbred served a dual purpose when racing against the clock. As such, throughout the 1960s and 1970s, the Thoroughbred was the quintessential horse show mount.

It was for this reason that young horsewoman Meredith McLaughlin made the trek from Southern Pines, North Carolina, to Lexington in the early months of 1968. McLaughlin, now a highly respected horse show judge and a legendary figure in the hunter/jumper world, was a newcomer to the auction scene when she made her first trip to Keeneland. McLaughlin was in search of a four-year-old that would serve to become a successful show hunter. Youth notwithstanding, McLaughlin possessed all the tools she needed for the task at hand: a good eye for a horse, a wealth of knowledge and the patience to develop a young prospect into a show ring champion.

On that brisk day, the sales pavilion was brimming with horses of all ages and jam-packed with would-be owners in search of their next prospect. Outside, rows of parked horse trailers formed a procession, their gleaming rigs shining against the rising sun. Inside the pavilion, bays, chestnuts and dappled greys were buffed and groomed and plaited with precision. There, in the midst of these Derby hopefuls, McLaughlin's eyes were drawn to a young chestnut colt.

The colt was, as McLaughlin recalls, "breathtakingly beautiful" and was as flawlessly groomed as any potential Derby winner. His copper coat shone like a newly minted coin, and his flaxen mane and tail had been combed to perfection. The horse stood less than sixteen hands, with near-perfect conformation built upon strong legs and hindquarters. He had a kind and curious eye that showed a small amount of white, which, as McLaughlin stood to the side of him, he rolled back at her as if to take a closer look. His face bore a white blaze that added to his elegant look, coupled with one stocking on his left hind leg.

As the horse was led through the sales pavilion, the auctioneer described him as a two-year-old Thoroughbred sired by Landman out of the mare Sandy Atlas. Landman hailed from the Nearco line, an important link in the pedigrees of many sport horses. The bidding lines opened, and McLaughlin promptly raised her hand to place a bid on the handsome young colt. When no higher offers appeared, the auctioneer slammed his gavel down and ordered McLaughlin to sign her ticket. She was now the new owner of the colt called San Man.

With her purchase in tow, McLaughlin was approached by the horse's breeder, a kindly, well-dressed older gentleman by the name of William Manis. The owner of a local family restaurant, Manis bred one Thoroughbred each year at his rural farm in Illinois. Manis proudly showed off some snapshots of the horse in younger days, standing beside his dam, being loaded into the trailer and nibbling small tufts of hay from Manis's own hand. In speaking with Manis, it was apparent to McLaughlin that the man took a great amount of pride in his animals. San Man's outer beauty was not only the product of the horse's genetics but also of Manis's diligent care and grooming.

As McLaughlin packed up her trailer and prepared for the journey to North Carolina, Manis mentioned that he had another young Thoroughbred back home in Illinois. The colt was, in fact, a half brother to San Man, having been foaled out of Sandy Atlas by Blazing Count, a son of the legendary Count Fleet. Impressed by the condition of San Man and Manis's apparent dedication to his animals, McLaughlin made a mental note.

After returning home to Southern Pines, McLaughlin promptly tacked up the unbroken colt. As the young horsewoman climbed aboard his back, she was taken by San Man's kind and quiet disposition. Despite being only two years old, the colt seemed to have not a care in the world. He was, as McLaughlin recalls after a lifetime of training horses, "an absolute dream" to ride and handle. This sentiment was echoed by McLaughlin's close friend Joey Darby, one of the leading professional hunter trainers and riders of the time. Darby, a friend of McLaughlin's since the two had been teenagers, would assist McLaughlin with San Man's training.

As San Man was preparing for his debut in the hunter ring, McLaughlin received an envelope in the mail from William Manis. Within the package were some snapshots of San Man's younger half brother, Sandsablaze, a bright chestnut colt with fancy white markings. Manis informed the young trainer of his plans to bring Sandsablaze to Keeneland, where he would be offered for sale at auction. As such, when January rolled around, McLaughlin found herself back in Lexington at the Keeneland sales pavilion.

Aside from a shared chestnut color and a white blaze, there was little resemblance between the two half brothers. Unlike San Man, who was almost perfectly conformed at two years old, Sandsablaze resembled an

Sandsablaze's half brother, San Man, is shown here with owner Meredith McLaughlin. *Photo courtesy of Meredith McLaughlin.*

awkward teenager. While McLaughlin remembers that Sandsablaze was "cute" and had a sweet, quiet disposition, he was, as Darby would later recall, "nothing but legs." The colt was exceptionally lanky, with a ewe neck, lop ears and a head that appeared too large for his frame. McLaughlin, however, was unfazed by the young colt's awkward appearance. The horse would likely grow into his body, and his fancy white markings would turn heads in the show ring. Without a second thought, McLaughlin purchased Sandsablaze and brought him home to Southern Pines—an area brimming with horse stables and endless bridle paths.

Like his half brother, Sandsablaze possessed a quiet disposition and quickly settled into his new surroundings. Under the care and training of McLaughlin, the colt slowly began to mature and was easily broken to saddle and bridle. At that time in history, Southern Pines was still a small community in which the residents—mostly equestrians—were familiar with one another. One of the most well-known area horsemen was William Ozelle "Pappy" Moss, a tall, sturdily built man with a soft spot for Thoroughbreds. Moss and

31

his wife, former southern belle Virginia Walthour "Ginnie" Moss, trained, foxhunted and showed Thoroughbreds at their Mile Away Farm, named for its proximity to the Southern Pines train station. The couple had been married since 1934, having met, rather fittingly, at a local horse show. Three years later, they established their farm, settling into a two-room apartment over the stable.

Pappy and Ginnie Moss shared a deep and undying love for horses, which would remain the primary focus of their lives. In fact, rather than traveling to an exotic location, they spent their honeymoon at a series of local horse shows. The Mosses often purchased and trained horses off the racetrack, developing them into foxhunters or show mounts for their many students. In 1942, Pappy became the master of the Moore County Hounds, one of the oldest hunts in North Carolina. As active participants in the foxhunting scene, the Mosses worked tirelessly to acquire enough land to ensure the future of the sport in Southern Pines. The end result, decades later, was the Walthour-Moss Foundation, which secured more than four thousand acres of land on which equestrians may ride and drive.

Having spent a lifetime training Thoroughbreds, Pappy Moss had a good eye for a horse. On one occasion, Moss and his friend Lloyd Tate were visiting McLaughlin's barn when Moss noticed the young Sandsablaze in his stall. Moss was immediately drawn to the now-gelded horse with the fancy markings and quiet demeanor. The hunt master felt that Sandsablaze would likely grow tall and thus become a suitable foxhunter. Moss purchased the lanky gelding from McLaughlin, with thoughts of riding the eye-catching horse on local hunts. Unfortunately for Moss, the horse did not grow as he had expected, and the huntsman soon concurred that the horse was too small for his needs. Moss decided to send Sandsablaze, whom stablehands had nicknamed "Pappy" in his honor, to be trained under the skillful hand of Joey Darby.

Now a legendary figure in the sport and a member of the Show Hunter Hall of Fame, Darby was at that time one of the leading riders of show hunters and jumpers on the East Coast. He was well known for his sense of style and seemed to possess a knack for bringing out the best in young horses. In the late 1960s, Darby had established his Any Day Farm in Southern Pines and was a frequent competitor at area shows. He trained and rode for many loyal horse owners, including the legendary Sally Sexton and Junie Kulp, and earned numerous championships in the show ring aboard both hunters and jumpers. Among the many horses he rode were future legends of the show ring, such as Showdown, Goodness and Balalaika.

Decades after their time together, Darby remembers the young Sandsablaze with pride. "Pappy was an incredible little horse," he recalls. "He was a very good boy who was always willing to try hard." As he had with San Man, Darby taught the little Thoroughbred to jump and noted that the horse took to it easily, despite his habit of rubbing fences with his front legs. He was not an easily spooked animal and was thus unfazed by the loud sounds and whirlwind activity that one would encounter at a horse show. Many young Thoroughbreds would balk at such activity, but Sandsablaze seemed to take it all in stride.

In an effort to gain some experience for the young horse, Darby trailered him to Upperville in Virginia for a horse show. The Upperville Colt and Horse Show, which traces its roots back to the late 1800s, showcased some of the top hunters and jumpers over a five-day period. Sandsablaze was entered in several classes over the course of the show; however, according to Darby, the young horse had other plans. When Darby checked on the horse in the mid-morning hours, he found young Sandsablaze lying flat in his stall, covered head to tail in bedding. Concerned that this was not normal behaviour for a young show horse, Darby summoned the veterinarian to examine Sandsablaze. "There was nothing wrong with him," Darby remembers. "He was growing and just liked to sleep." Indeed, this act of sleeping during shows would become one of Sandsablaze's later trademarks.

CHAPTER 4
EARLY YEARS

In the spring of 1970, Joey Darby brought Sandsablaze to a local show hosted by the Tryon Riding & Hunt Club in an effort to showcase the horse to an audience of potential buyers. The horse show was held at Harmon Field, a multi-acre grass parcel in Tryon, another equestrian area in North Carolina. At that time, there were no "pre-green" or "schooling" hunter classes in which to introduce a young horse to the show ring. As such, Darby entered Sandsablaze in the first-year green hunter division, where the jumps were set at three feet, six inches.

As Darby skillfully guided Sandsablaze around the outside course, a young woman by the name of Sally Walker was ringside, awaiting her turn aboard her own young prospect. Having grown up in Tryon as a competitive equestrienne, Walker knew Darby well. They often competed at the same shows, and Walker enjoyed watching Darby tackle a course with the flair that had become his trademark. In this instance, however, it was the horse Darby was riding that commanded the young woman's attention.

Walker was surprised at her own level of interest in the young gelding, as she was not in the market for another show horse. She had recently sold her beloved Thoroughbred Polk County, a son of the Argentinian champion Thoroughbred Setubal out of Stella Polaris, a granddaughter of the legendary Man o' War. While embarking on a promising career in advertising, Walker no longer had the time to travel to horse shows all over the East Coast; instead, she would focus on training young prospects at home. Besides that fact, Walker reminded herself, she was never a

Joey Darby advertised Sandsablaze for sale in March 1970 in the *Chronicle of the Horse*. *Photo reprinted with permission of the* Chronicle of the Horse.

great fan of chestnuts, particularly those adorned with white such as the one Darby was riding. Nevertheless, Walker sensed there was something special about this horse.

As the day progressed, Walker's mind could not release the image of the leggy Sandsablaze, who, she remembers, "cruised around in a ground-covering stride and jumped every jump with those white knees neatly folded in a square." Walker felt that the horse "clearly had more talent than all the rest of the class combined." Despite the fact that her own mount had earned a higher ribbon than Sandsablaze in the class, Walker believed that the little chestnut was something special. Soon she found herself making her way over to speak with Darby and inquire as to whether the animal was for sale.

Darby informed her that Sandsablaze was indeed available and that he was owned by Pappy and Ginnie Moss, with whom Walker was familiar. In no time, a deal was made. Walker remembers, "Joey made a call, and before you knew it, I had bought the flashy chestnut." At the time of the purchase, Sandsablaze had been slated to compete at the Devon Horse Show in Pennsylvania, the highlight of the early summer show season on the East Coast. As Darby had already made arrangements to show Sandsablaze at Devon, Walker gave him her blessing. Due to her career commitments, however, she was unable to accompany them on the trip.

Sandsablaze earned a low ribbon or two at Devon, but he had not yet grown into his true potential. While he showed glimmers of style in the hunter ring, he was still green and coltish at times and showed a tendency to be lazy over the jumps. His legs were often uneven in front, and he characteristically rubbed the tops of fences, leading Darby to believe that the horse would never jump higher than three feet, six inches. "I don't think he wowed anyone," Walker recalled of his showing at Devon. Nevertheless, both Darby and Walker were pleased with young Sandsablaze's progress.

After Devon, Walker opted to give the horse some time off to mature before resuming his training in the fall. Sandsablaze, at three years old, was still "all legs," which resulted in a lack of surefootedness over uneven terrain. Like many young Thoroughbreds, he simply needed time to mature. With this in mind, Walker arranged for the shipper to drop Sandsablaze off in Virginia for several weeks of rest and relaxation.

The time spent at pasture served young Sandsablaze well. At summer's end, Walker hauled the horse back to Tryon, where she leased two stalls from trainers Gerald and Betsy Pack at Comoco Farm. It was a "rough board" setup, in which Walker was required to feed and care for Sandsablaze and her other horse on a daily basis. "It was the next best thing to keeping him

The legendary Joey Darby was the first to show Sandsablaze. Here Darby pilots "Pappy" over a fence at the Devon Horse Show. *Photo courtesy of Joey Darby.*

at home," Walker later recalled. As the property was surrounded by trails, Walker often hacked Sandsablaze through the winding woods and bridle paths, which seemed to help the young horse gain a better of sense of his own footfalls. While the horse seemed to enjoy these hacks in the woods, his spirit came alive when Walker pointed him toward a jump. "He could and would jump anything, in the ring or on the trail," Walker remembers.

As an important part of Sandsablaze's training, Walker worked the horse on the flat as well as over fences, noting that he was "a lovely mover" boasting a fluid, ground-covering stride. With his quiet disposition, nice movement and apparent fondness for jumping, Walker felt that the horse had the makings of an amateur owner hunter.

While Sandsablaze was quiet and well mannered on the ground, he was not, by any means, a barnyard pet. Walker remembers that he could be "snitty" or "fussy" in his stall, noting that the horse preferred not to be coddled. "He was in no way a cuddly horse," she said. "He would accept face stroking as if it were his due, not because he liked my loving touch. So he probably had the pro mentality from the beginning." As she did with all her horses, however, Walker taught Sandsablaze to bow on command by stretching his head down between his knees. "He liked to perform, and I think in some way he understood accolades for a job well done," she said.

Since his early days with Pappy Moss, Sandsablaze had always been informally known by his master's namesake. Upon arrival at the Packs' farm, however, the horse was in need of another barn name, albeit on a temporary basis. Betsy Pack had a horse of her own named "Pappy" (also purchased from the Mosses), and having two horses with the same name quickly led to undue confusion. Walker therefore opted to call Sandsablaze "Stilts" because, as she remembers, the horse "looked like he was walking on four white stilts." With affection, she addressed him by the nickname "Stiltsy."

The town of Tryon was situated in the midst of foxhunting country; its emerald fields and woods made riding to hounds a fashionable activity. One of the most popular hunts took place on Thanksgiving Day, and as the hunt was held right down the street from the barn, Walker figured this to be a good opportunity to introduce Sandsablaze to foxhunting. Unfortunately for Walker, the presence of the hounds and whirlwind of commotion led the young horse to become agitated.

"While everyone was gathering before the hounds were let out, my horse spent the entire time leaping in the air and whirling around," Walker remembers. "When the field took off, he went ballistic and decided to ride home instead of barreling after the hunt. Foxhunting was clearly not his calling."

By now, the weather had turned cool and the trees had gone bare as winter made its way to Tryon. In an effort to escape the winter doldrums, Walker decided to accompany the Packs to Tampa, Florida, for a series of horse shows. Walker brought Sandsablaze along, while the Packs brought their own horses, Bronze and Pappy. Walker did not have a trainer at the time but felt that, with no pressure or goals in mind, the experience would be an enjoyable way to escape the barren winter. "I had not planned to have another show horse," she said, "but this one was just too talented to sit at home and just go on the trail."

The decision proved to be a good one. Walker put in a fabulous trip to win her first amateur owner class aboard the chestnut, defeating several more experienced horses and riders. Also present at the show was Walker's friend Meredith McLaughlin, the young trainer who had originally purchased Sandsablaze at Keeneland. McLaughlin was thrilled to see how much

Sally Walker showed Sandsablaze successfully in the amateur owner hunter divisions. *Photo by Bob Foster, courtesy of Sally Walker.*

Sandsablaze had developed and telephoned Joey Darby at her earliest convenience to share the good news with him.

Walker remembers that she let her nerves get the best of her after the first class, but the horse performed well enough to earn reserve championship honors. Walker recalls that she could ask the horse for any distance and he would take it willingly, right or wrong. He also earned a ribbon in the under saddle or "hack" class because he had a lovely step with "fabulous ground-covering strides."

Walker was impressed with Sandsablaze's performance in Tampa, so much so that she began to do some solid thinking about the gelding's future. The horse had talent, but with a busy career, Walker simply did not have the time to bring him to horse shows on a regular basis. More than anything, she wanted the horse to be able to reach his full potential in the show ring, as she felt he was too talented to be used solely as a trail horse. Soon she decided to offer Sandsablaze for sale.

With no potential buyers on the horizon, Walker opted to gain some exposure for Sandsablaze by campaigning him at a few more shows. Their first stop was Upperville, the show he had attended—but slept through—the year before with Joey Darby. Now, a year later, he was ready to shine. Competing in both the second-year green and amateur owner divisions, Walker remembers that Sandsablaze was "quite spectacular," earning top ribbons in good competition against well-known riders and trainers. Walker recalls that Sandsablaze jumped "magnificently" at Upperville, sans trainer, turning some heads in the process but without gaining a buyer.

It was then off to Connecticut for Ox Ridge and Fairfield, two of the premier horse shows on the East Coast. "By this time, the jumps were so easy for Sandsablaze that he started to anticipate and get a bit cranked up around the outside courses, which were lovely and long," Walker remembers. "He got some decent ribbons nevertheless. Jumping was totally effortless for him."

When still no buyer appeared for the flashy chestnut, Walker approached Bob Freels, whose client Gladys Busk had purchased her beloved Polk County. Busk, a Greenwich horsewoman and mother of four, was now dominating the amateur owner divisions with Polk County; the pair would go on to capture AHSA horse of the year honors in that division.

Bob Freels and his wife, Jeri, operated Harkaway Farm in Greenwich, Connecticut, where they trained some of the leading amateur and junior hunter riders on the East Coast. Freels's knowledge was immense, having served as the manager for the U.S. Equestrian Team, and he was skilled at bringing out the best in both horses and riders. He taught his clients that horsemanship began from the ground up; Freels's riders were well known for the care and treatment of their animals in addition to their time in the saddle. Walker thought that perhaps Freels could find a suitable buyer for Sandsablaze. Initially, Freels was a bit concerned about the horse's immaturity, as many juniors and amateurs required more experienced, or "made," horses.

Yet there was one rider, Freels believed, who likely could handle Sandsablaze's quirks while refining his raw jumping ability. This rider, whom Freels had known for years, was a boy with a deep and lasting admiration for horses. At just fifteen years old, this boy had a larger amount of talent and perseverance than many older and more experienced riders. His ability to showcase a horse's talent had become so well known in the area that he was often called upon as a "catch rider" who would climb aboard an unfamiliar mount and show the animal over a course of fences. Besides being a "natural" on a horse's back, he was an exceptionally hard worker with the patience to bring along a young, green prospect.

Sally Walker and Sandsablaze clear a fence at a horse show in Tampa. *Photo by Meredith McLaughlin, courtesy of Sally Walker.*

The rider to whom Freels referred was currently showing his Thoroughbred gelding, Sourball, to great success in the small junior hunter division, which was open to horses measuring up to 16.0 hands in height. In order to also compete in the large junior hunters, the boy's family was in the market for a slightly taller horse. At 15.3½ hands at the withers and still in the midst of an apparent growth spurt, Sandsablaze seemed to fit the bill. A deal was made, and at the June 1971 Fairfield Horse Show, Sandsablaze was introduced to young Buddy Brown.

CHAPTER 5
LIKE FATHER, LIKE SON

R iding a horse," wrote Ralph Waldo Emerson, "is not a gentle hobby, to be picked up and laid down like a game of solitaire. It is a grand passion. It seizes a person whole and once it has done so, he will have to accept that his life will be radically changed."

For William "Buddy" Brown, that passion for horses had begun early. As a child, he was gifted with a natural ability to bring out the best in any horse, giving the animal a deep sense of security while guiding it over a course of fences. That innate ability to form a partnership with a horse stemmed from a genuine love for all equines. Size, color or breed did not matter; Buddy Brown simply adored horses.

William Vincent Brown came into the world on Friday, April 13, 1956, as the second of five children born to Graham and Pattie (Primavera) Brown. The Browns' original plan was to call their new son Billy; however, older brother Skip, like many toddlers, had difficulty enunciating the letter "l." Rather than pronouncing the name "Billy," Skip called his baby brother what sounded more like "Buddy." From then on, young William would always be known as Buddy Brown. Two years after Buddy's birth, the family would expand to include a sister, Leslie. Two more children, Stephen and Meghan, would follow years later.

When asked what sparked young Buddy's interest in horses, his father, Graham, would jokingly admit that he "was to blame." The elder Brown, in fact, had loved horses for as long as he could remember. This horse passion had set hold back in the years of the Great Depression, when Graham was a toddler in Darien, Connecticut. While his mother worked in New York City to help support the family, Graham was looked after by his maternal grandfather. The older man's job was to deliver grain to local farms, most of which housed a steady supply of workhorses. Graham recalled the touch of the soft, velvety muzzles; the warmth of a horse's breath against his young face; and the feeling of empowerment when placed atop the back of a sturdy equine. In those early moments, a true affinity for horses was created.

As the years passed and Graham became older, the opportunity arose to nurture his passion a bit more. At the age of ten, Graham's neighborhood friend, who suffered from a disability, was signed up for horseback riding lessons as a method of therapy. Young Graham often accompanied his friend to such lessons, where he was able to observe the intricacies of learning to ride. By the age of fourteen, he had demonstrated enough aptitude for the sport to be hired by a local hacking stable that took would-be riders on guided tours. In exchange for mucking stalls and tacking up horses, Brown was able to lead weekend riders through the wooded trails and fields that surrounded the stable.

The elder Brown was able to ride a bit throughout his teenage years but was never afforded the opportunity to have a horse of his own. As a young man, Brown married his high school sweetheart, Pattie, and the couple moved to a small apartment in New York City. There was little time for horses at this time in Brown's life, as he worked his way through college, studying industrial design. He was hired as a draftsman for Pattie's family's foundry business and would eventually work his way up to company president.

As their family expanded, Graham and Pattie constructed a house in Darien, Connecticut, a section of Fairfield County known for its equestrian properties. There, Graham was able to indulge his love of horses, often riding through the local hills and fields with an equestrian friend. By the time of the birth of the Browns' fourth child, Steve, in February 1961, Graham decided it was time to purchase a horse of his own. He soon acquired a Canadian hunter gelding by the name of Shorty, who resembled an undersized Clydesdale, albeit with a roached mane. Shorty was boarded at Denwood Stables in Stamford, Connecticut.

From Denwood Stables, a short hack through the woods led to the grounds where the Fairfield-Westchester Professional Horsemen's Association (PHA) show was held each June. Roughly five months after purchasing Shorty, Brown attended his first horse show as a spectator. It was there, Brown recalls, that he set his eyes on some "long legged beauties"—tall, elegant Thoroughbreds who floated effortlessly across the ground. After watching these horses jump with ease over the rolling outside course, Brown decided that he had to have a Thoroughbred of his own.

Brown headed to Kauffman & Sons, a well-known tack shop in Manhattan, to obtain some information as to where he could find some Thoroughbreds for sale. At the recommendation of a local horseman, he visited the stable of Tanya Forman, who bred Thoroughbreds at her New Jersey farm. Brown photographed Forman's two-year-olds as they frolicked in the paddocks and, upon returning to Denwood Stables, presented the snapshots to stable owner Bryce Orville Davies. The latter, described as a "wily Welshman," carefully examined each photograph, ultimately giving a two-year-old filly his stamp of approval. With Davies's blessing, Brown purchased the yet-unbroken filly and had her shipped to Denwood Stables.

The filly, Live Ice, was a kindly animal that took well to Brown's gentle hand. She allowed Brown to approach her while she was lying down in her stall and, in time, to drape his weight across her back. Under Davies's supervision, Brown worked hard at ground-training the filly, utilizing various long-line exercises to gain her trust and establish control. On one occasion, Davies instructed Brown to tack up the filly, and the two men proceeded to hand-walk her one mile to the local show grounds. Once there, Davies told Brown to turn the filly ten times to the right, then ten circles to the left and, finally, to climb aboard her back. The horse responded well to his aids; in no time, Brown was trotting and then cantering the young animal.

Brown "played," as he says, with the filly all summer, even entering a flat class at a local show in Greenwich the following autumn. When it was decided that the filly required additional training, Brown contacted noted horseman Victor Hugo-Vidal in Stamford, Connecticut. Live Ice was shipped to Hugo-Vidal's historic Cedar Lodge Farm, where the trainer schooled the horse on weekdays while Brown worked in Manhattan. On the weekends, Brown would take lessons from Hugo-Vidal, riding some of the trainer's school horses in order to hone his jumping skills. When Brown realized that he required a more seasoned mount, a sale ad for Live Ice was placed in the local paper. Trainer Artie Hawkins, responding to the ad, purchased Live Ice as a racing prospect. The filly would go on to achieve considerable success on the track, winning a feature race at Florida's Gulfstream Park.

As Brown became further involved in the local horse scene, he became a member of the Ox Ridge Hunt Club, a premier equestrian facility located not far from the family's home in Darien. The property had originally been established in 1914 by opera singer John McCormick, who had operated it as a dairy farm. By the 1960s, the farm was under the management of the famous trainer Otto Heuckeroth, whose past students included icons such as George Morris, Ronnie Mutch and Brown's instructor Victor Hugo-Vidal. In addition to its training and boarding options, the club hosted several horse shows on its grounds, including the Ox Ridge Charity Horse Show, held each year in early June. Through the years, the show would attract the best competitors in the hunter and jumper divisions, including a slew of international riders and their mounts.

During his early years at Ox Ridge, Graham Brown purchased a bay Thoroughbred gelding that he called Shantytown. While the horse was not a particularly good mover, he excelled at jumping, and Brown rode the horse with some success in the first-year green hunter division at several local shows in the summer of 1964. Brown realized that because of Shantytown's choppy movement, the horse was not going to shine at the highly competitive "A" shows; therefore, the pair headed instead to the one-day "B" shows. At the Bethlehem, Connecticut summer show in August, Brown decided to switch over from the hunters to the jumper ring. The pair was entered in four classes, winning three low ribbons, a bit of prize money and, to Brown's astonishment, the PHA class. Later that

Buddy's father, Graham Brown, was also an accomplished horseman. Here he is shown on the Thoroughbred Shantytown at the Fairfield Horse Show. *Photo courtesy of Graham Brown.*

Graham Brown is shown here aboard one of his other mounts, Bag of Tricks, at Ox Ridge in the late 1960s. *Photo courtesy of Graham and Buddy Brown.*

Graham Brown and Shantytown at the Boulder Brook Horse Show. *Photo courtesy of Graham and Buddy Brown.*

summer, Brown sold Shantytown to Brian Flynn, who was still a junior, to be used as his mount at the equitation finals.

In the years that followed, as the elder Brown continued to progress in his riding, he and Pattie converted a greenhouse on their property into a two-stall barn, renovating the surrounding area to include turnout paddocks and a riding ring. Brown also purchased several different horses, including a gelding called Bag of Tricks, and enjoyed showing them in local hunter classes. By this time, as Skip and Buddy were old enough to begin riding, the family bought a grey Shetland pony called Soapsuds for the children to enjoy.

Like most little boys, young Buddy Brown enjoyed pretending to be a cowboy, and with the addition of "Soapy" to the family, he now had a pony to help play the part. Buddy recalls wearing his cowboy hat and fringed vest while he rode Soapy around the family's farm. Like most little ponies, Soapy could be a bit of a rogue and often took young Buddy on wild rides around the property. On one occasion, as Buddy rode in the local town parade while dressed as Paul Revere, Soapy decided that he had had enough of the Fourth of July festivities. The pony galloped back to the barn, jumping stone walls and puddles along the way as young Buddy grabbed his mane and held on for dear life. After having enough of such pony antics, Buddy decided to quit riding and play Little League baseball instead. That interest in ballgames was short-lived, however, and Brown soon returned, unequivocally, to his beloved horses. The "grand passion" for horses had begun to take hold, and Buddy Brown's young life was about to be radically changed.

CHAPTER 6

DERBY HILL

By the time Buddy was ten years old, it had become clear that the young boy had a unique talent for equestrian sports. He had fast become one of the top "pony jocks" in the area, winning numerous championships aboard his small chestnut pony, Sparkler, whom his father had purchased from a local farm. Buddy enjoyed cantering "Sparky" over fence after fence, often raising the height of the jumps when nobody was watching.

Around this time, Graham and Pattie moved their family from Darien, Connecticut, to South Salem, New York, where they purchased a colonial farm by the name of Derby Hill—a fitting name for a family that loved Thoroughbred horses. Derby Hill was part of a parcel that had originally spanned more than thirty acres; the twenty acres that remained would provide ample room for the family's growing band of horses. The Browns built a four-stall barn on the property, along with several paddocks and a chute for free-longing horses over jumps. Later, the barn would be vastly expanded to include more than twenty stalls.

The daily maintenance of the barn and horses was a chore shared by all family members. The children were responsible for the care of their horses and ponies, which included mucking stalls and feeding and grooming the animals. After school, Buddy and his siblings would rush home to complete their chores in anticipation of a ride on their favorite horse or pony. As Buddy and his sister Leslie were particularly interested in showing, Pattie often drove them to Secor Farms Riding Club in White Plains, New York, where they took lessons from Wayne Carroll on the farm's school horses.

As a young boy, Buddy Brown was a top pony rider. Here he is shown aboard his small pony, Sparkler, at Ox Ridge in 1966. *Photo courtesy of Buddy Brown.*

Upon returning home to Derby Hill, Buddy and Leslie would practice these lessons on their own horses and ponies.

Young Buddy Brown was a rising star in the show ring, piloting his pony calmly and stylishly over fences and on the flat. As he collected blue ribbons at various East Coast horse shows, a woman by the name of Wilhelmine Waller was watching from ringside. She was the wife of Tom Waller, a well-known area trainer and breeder of racehorses. The Wallers bred both Thoroughbreds and hunter ponies at their 250-acre Tanrackin Farm in Bedford, New York. Known affectionately as the "Grand Dame of Bedford," Mrs. Waller had developed a line of fancy show ponies by crossing her Thoroughbred stallion, Chantain, with small pony mares she had imported from Wales. The ponies were ridden and shown by Mrs. Waller's young goddaughter, Meta Boykin.

As is the case with growing children, Boykin soon became too tall for the ponies, leaving Mrs. Waller to search for a younger and smaller show rider. After watching Buddy dominate the small pony hunter division with Sparkler, Mrs. Waller questioned local trainer Artie Hawkins as to the name

Buddy Brown and his pony, Sparkler, clear a fence at Fairfield in 1967. *Photo courtesy of Buddy Brown.*

Buddy Brown's success with his pony, Sparkler, earned the attention of pony breeder Wilhelmine Waller. *Photo courtesy of Buddy Brown.*

of the child. Mrs. Waller was soon introduced to the Brown family, and it was arranged for Buddy to begin riding the Tanrackin Farm ponies. As the highly bred ponies were much more spirited than his own Sparkler, Buddy received valuable instruction from his trainer Wayne Carroll on how to bring out their best in the show ring. Buddy experienced great success with the Tanrackin Farm ponies, which included the noted champion Welland Valley Early Bird. With Early Bird, Buddy earned championship honors at the National Horse Show in 1967, the last year in which the pony divisions were offered at the old Madison Square Garden. (Incidentally, the pony hunter divisions would not return to the National Horse Show for another twenty-seven years.)

When Buddy outgrew the smaller mounts, the Browns acquired a large pony by the name of Wennol Bechan (aka Becky), whom they had first seen at the Devon Horse Show in Pennsylvania. At that time in history, there was no medium pony hunter division; Becky, at a solid 13.1 hands, was thus shown as a large pony. The pony was owned at that time by a Mrs. Cox from Boston, Massachusetts, and was under the care of Virginia horseman Clay T. "Barney" Brittle. Becky was being ridden at Devon by Barney's young son, Skip Brittle, who would later earn fame as a champion steeplechase jockey. Young Skip virtually chased the pony around Devon's famous ovals, with the reins flapping wildly over each and every jump; nevertheless, the pair managed to win a ribbon in every class.

With the idea of finding a large pony that could win at the big shows, Graham Brown approached the senior Brittle and learned that Becky was indeed for sale. A deal was agreed upon in which the Browns would take the pony back home to Derby Hill for a pre-purchase veterinary exam. The family's vet at that time was Howard Raven, DVM, who was well-known around Fairfield County as a "real horseman's vet." When Doc Raven first saw Becky move, he noted that she would be a winner in the show ring. Time proved that Raven's opinion was indeed correct.

Wayne Carroll, who was Buddy's trainer at the time, was not quite as impressed with the pony. Carroll noted when he first saw Becky that the pony was unlikely to ever win a model class. However, with the proper exercise, grooming and feeding, she went on to win such classes on numerous occasions. It must be mentioned that, at this time in history, the acquisition of Wennol Bechan was of great importance. In every respect, Becky was a miniature Thoroughbred, having been sired by a Welsh stallion out of a Princequillo mare. With the sensitivity of a finely tuned Thoroughbred, Wennol Bechan taught Buddy the finesse necessary to guide a Thoroughbred around a hunter course in winning fashion. Becky won numerous championships with Buddy in the saddle (and later with Buddy's sister Leslie) and captured the prestigious Gregory Beowulf Saunders Trophy two years in a row. During all the years in which the Browns showed her, Becky never competed at more than twelve shows per year. The experience with Becky was a major contributing factor in making Buddy the tremendously successful hunter rider that he became as both a junior and, later, an adult.

In 1967, Graham Brown accompanied Artie Hawkins to a sale at New York's Belmont Park, where he found the horse that was to become Buddy's next show hunter. The horse, Sourball, was a handsome mahogany bay with a crooked blaze and four white socks. He was a son of the race champion Ridan out of the mare Lemon Souffle but had been held back from the track after developing a case of bucked shins. The elder Brown purchased the horse for the sum of $1,800 and brought him home to Derby Hill with the sale ticket still affixed to Sourball's hindquarters.

On a rainy Sunday afternoon, Graham Brown tacked up young Sourball and led him by a lead shank around the paddock. The horse was so quiet that Graham soon put young Buddy, then eleven years old, in the saddle and led the pair in a circle on the grounds of Derby Hill. Later, in the jumping chute, the horse showed natural ability; he jumped, as Graham recalled,

Buddy Brown and Wennol Bechan, shown here at Fairfield in 1968, were highly successful in the large pony hunter division. *Photo courtesy of Graham and Buddy Brown.*

"with his knees up to his ears." Noting the horse's quiet disposition and talent for jumping, Brown sent Sourball to North Carolina to train over the winter with professional rider Jeri Freels. In early June, Graham brought Buddy and Skip to North Carolina for a week to observe the horse in training with Jeri. The following season, the horse returned to Derby Hill, where Jeri showed Sourball in the first-year green classes and young Buddy rode him in the junior classes, winning countless blue ribbons and trophies. In the next few years, Brown and Sourball would dominate the small junior hunter division.

While Buddy and Sourball continued with great success in the small juniors, Graham was on the lookout for a large junior hunter for his son to show. At the barn of a New Jersey trainer, they found The Swede, a strapping bay Thoroughbred that had recently been imported from Europe. A fancy mover with suspension in his gaits, the solidly built gelding had competed successfully in the sport of dressage. With his lovely way of moving and handsome looks, it seemed as if The Swede had the makings of a successful show hunter. Graham Brown named the horse "Polkagris"—the Swedish word for hard candy—as a tribute to Sourball.

Talent aside, Polkagris lacked the quiet disposition that characterizes a winning junior hunter. He also did not take well to jumping. The horse was flighty at shows and was difficult to settle in the ring; in between classes, he paced nervously in his stall. In an effort to calm the horse, Buddy rode Polkagris on nearby trails and bridle paths. Ironically, in the wide-open spaces, with wildlife and nature all around him, the fidgety horse seemed to be at ease. He enjoyed being ridden through the woods and seemed to take on an air of calmness. A career in the show ring as a junior hunter was simply not the horse's calling.

Realizing that Polkagris was not a suitable show mount for his son, Graham Brown continued on his quest for a large junior hunter. In late spring, Bob and Jeri Freels informed the elder Brown about a sale horse called Sandsablaze that seemed to have the exact qualities that Polkagris lacked. Sandsablaze was unflappable in the ring and appeared to have a strong fondness for jumping. Graham Brown, who had observed Sandsablaze at a few local shows with Joey Darby, agreed that the horse might be a good match for Buddy. A deal was made whereby Brown and Sally Walker would essentially trade horses, with additional payment made to Walker to account for the higher price for Sandsablaze. The deal was finalized at the Fairfield Horse Show in June 1971, and Sandsablaze became the new mount for young Buddy Brown.

CHAPTER 7
A PARTNERSHIP BEGINS

Any horseman worth his salt knows the value of a "horse of a lifetime." A horse in this category may not always be the most talented of the lot but forges with its rider an unbreakable bond. While movies and novels often portray an instant, karmic connection between horse and human, a true partnership in real life typically takes time to develop. In the case of Sandsablaze, Brown recalls that he had no real expectations when he first set his eyes on the leggy chestnut. In fact, there was little indication at that point that the horse would take young Brown on the ride of his life.

After being acquired in June by the Browns, Sandsablaze adapted quickly to his new home at Derby Hill. That summer, he and Buddy began competing in the large junior hunter division, although Sandsablaze—at 15.3¾—barely made the 16.0-hand cutoff. On July 29, the pair won the stake class and placed second in the hack to earn championship honors at Fairfield's midsummer horse show. Brown and "Pappy's" eight total points secured the tricolor, while Anne Whitehead's Double Meaning was named reserve champion. This win was memorable only because it propelled Sandsablaze to his first major news headline. The *New York Times* proclaimed in bold lettering in its July 30 edition, "Junior Working Title Goes to Sandsablaze in Westport."

This victory notwithstanding, Sandsablaze's success as a junior hunter was limited by his tendency to rub fences and jump unevenly with his front end. While these minor glitches were not huge factors in local events, the added competition at the top-recognized horse shows was enough to keep

Sandsablaze from consistently winning classes. The junior hunter division was, and is, supremely competitive, with many talented and experienced horses vying for the top prizes. "He had limited success," Brown later recalled of Sandsablaze's stint in the junior hunters. "He wasn't horrible at it, and he wasn't great at it."[4]

Robin Rost (now Fairclough), a top junior rider at that same time, remembers watching Brown ride Sandsablaze in these early days. Rost recalls that Brown was excited to show Pappy to his friends, as the young riders had a strong camaraderie and enjoyed getting to know the new horses on the circuit. Fairclough's first impression was that Sandsablaze was a good jumper but, as Joey Darby had suggested earlier, did not always appear to have classic hunter form. Fairclough recognized that Brown had to work extra hard to develop Sandsablaze into the champion he was to become. "It was highly impressive to see them work together," Fairclough, now a top trainer, recalls. "Buddy worked hard with that horse, and Sandsablaze became the exact horse that Buddy wanted." Fairclough would follow the pair in the years to come, noting that Brown's later success with Pappy was well beyond anyone's expectations at the time.

As Brown continued to show in the hunter divisions with Sandsablaze and other horses, his mind wandered to thoughts of competing in the jumper ring. The teen yearned for the higher fences and tighter courses of the jumper world, where style did not matter as much as height and speed. Brown often watched from ringside as his longtime idol, the incomparable Rodney Jenkins, skillfully cleared a course of huge fences in a thrilling race against the clock. Jenkins, known as the "Red Rider" due to his trademark ginger-colored locks, was among the most dominant equestrians of the era. With a style all his own and a positive attitude, he had the ability to make a course of imposing jumps appear fun and effortless. At the Washington International Horse Show in the fall, Brown watched as Jenkins and his mount, the legendary Thoroughbred Idle Dice, became the first pair in history to win the prestigious President's Cup twice in a row. For the teenaged Buddy Brown, riding in the jumper ring became a constant, driving ambition.

Brown soon informed his parents and trainer of his desire to compete in the jumper divisions. Trainer Bob Freels, who concentrated solely on hunters, suggested that Brown work with Olympian George H. Morris. Freels knew Morris well, having served as manager of the U.S. Equestrian Team (USET) when Morris rode in the Olympic Games. Morris's record in the sport was unmatched; he rode on eight winning Nations Cup teams between 1958 and 1960 alone and won a silver medal in the 1960 Olympic

Games. Widely regarded as the father of hunt seat riding, Morris trained numerous champions at his Hunterdon stable in Pittstown, New Jersey.

Freels arranged for the Browns to set up a meeting with Morris at the National Horse Show that fall in New York. During a break in between classes, Graham and Buddy Brown sat down for lunch with the legendary trainer. Recognizing Brown's natural talent, Morris agreed to take the boy on as a student and assist him in his quest toward competing in the jumpers. To gain some experience, Morris loaned Brown a veteran jumper called Big Line, who had won the open jumper championship at the National Horse Show with Conrad Homfeld in the saddle. There was one provision, however; in addition to jumpers, Brown would also have to compete in equitation classes.

For many junior riders, equitation classes serve as a stepping-stone to a career in the jumper ring. Unlike hunter classes, which are judged on the style of the horse, equitation places its emphasis on the rider. In equitation over fences, riders are judged on their ability to execute a course of jumps, demonstrating near-perfect form and style in their position. The equitation course is much more technical than a hunter round, and it might include rollback turns, narrow fences, various lead changes, long approaches and bending lines to test the rider's skill. The equitation rider should execute these movements using aids that are invisible to spectators.

Brown had little experience in equitation classes and, as he recalls, had an even smaller amount of interest. Riding an equitation class had little appeal to Brown, who yearned to ride fast around tight, twisting turns. He trusted the great trainer's judgment, however, as Morris knew the subject matter better than anyone. Morris's book, *Hunter Seat Equitation*, originally published in 1971, was—and remains—the definitive work on correct hunter seat riding. Having won both major equitation finals himself at the age of fourteen, Morris had since coached several riders to prominent equitation wins. Many of those students, including Conrad Homfeld, had since become leading riders in the grand prix ranks. Morris realized how valuable the experience of competing in equitation could be for a young rider such as Buddy Brown. Then, of course, the question arose as to which horse Brown would ride.

Back then, it was common for hunters to serve "double duty" in the equitation ring, as few riders had horses specifically for the equitation classes. However, Sourball could be spooky at times, and Big Line was the typical hot-tempered jumper. That, Brown recalls, left Sandsablaze as the only option.

"When George asked me what horse I could ride for equitation," Brown recalled, "I told him, 'I have this horse—Sandsablaze—who is a little clumsy, but he's done the hunters a bit, and he is not spooky.'" Morris responded that he would like to see the horse for himself. Only by observing Sandsablaze in action could Morris decide if the young chestnut would be up to the task.

CHAPTER 8
EQUITATION HORSE

In order to prepare for equitation classes, Buddy and Sandsablaze began lessons with Morris at his famed Hunterdon Stable. Long before dawn, while the city was asleep, Graham and Buddy would load Sandsablaze into the van for the two-hour drive from New York to New Jersey. The van was packed with all the necessary tack and supplies, ensuring that Sandsablaze would be well cared for during the long hours to come. This would become the Browns' Saturday morning routine on the weekends that Morris was not competing.

Lessons with Morris served as a bit of a culture shock for Buddy, who, up until this time, had never truly experienced a formal flatwork lesson. A mastery of flatwork is crucial when jumping fences, particularly a technical equitation or jumper course, where every stride is critical. Brown and Sandsablaze were thus introduced to a variety of unfamiliar movements, including dressage basics such as shoulder-in and leg yielding, to help make the horse supple and keep him working from behind. Brown recalls that the first time he was asked for "volte"—a very tight circle that serves as a balancing exercise for the horse—he had to ask Morris to explain what the word meant.

For Sandsablaze, as with Brown, equitation was a whole new world. "He really just got thrown into lessons," Brown recalls. "It was sink or swim." Some of their lessons would be private, with the pair garnering Morris's full attention; at other times, they would be part of a group lesson with other Hunterdon students, including future Olympians Melanie Smith and Katie

Monahan. Brown was mesmerized by the string of gorgeous horses in the stable at Hunterdon, all of which were groomed to perfection with flawlessly pulled manes and glossy coats. As Brown remembers, there was not a single horse on the property that was less than beautiful.

Buddy and Pappy worked hard on improving their flatwork, with Graham supervising their progress in between lessons with Morris. Sandsablaze's flat topline and unusual conformation, coupled with his natural sluggishness, made it difficult for Brown to get the horse working in a frame. Unlike most Thoroughbreds, who are naturally forward, Sandsablaze lacked impulsion and required a substantial amount of leg pressure from the rider to engage his hindquarters. This created an additional challenge for equitation classes, as it can be difficult to maintain a perfect position when riding a lazy horse that requires "a lot of leg."

While Morris was in Florida over the winter months, he instructed Brown to enter equitation classes at local shows in an effort to qualify for the finals held annually at indoors. Nowadays, riders have many options, as several different finals are held at the end of the annual show season. Back in the 1970s, however, when Buddy and Sandsablaze competed, there were only two from which to choose: the American Horse Shows Association (AHSA) (now USEF) Medal, known as "the Medal," and the American Society of the Prevention of Cruelty to Animals (ASPCA) Maclay, referred to simply as "the Maclay." The culmination of a successful equitation career was a win in the Medal or Maclay finals. An elite group of riders, including Morris (in 1952) and his student, Conrad Homfeld (in 1967), had won both finals in the same year.

Junior riders who have not celebrated their eighteenth birthday as of January 1 must qualify for the finals at a designated class during the show season. Typically, an equitation rider will begin by competing in "maiden" classes, which are open to riders who have not yet won a blue ribbon in equitation. From there, they will move up to novice classes, restricted to those who have won fewer than three blue ribbons. Limit classes are open to those with fewer than six blue ribbons. Typically, by the time a rider qualifies for a final, he or she has accumulated numerous blue ribbons in equitation and is classified as an "open" rider.

Buddy Brown qualified for the Medal finals at the Devon Horse Show in early June, which was a bit of an ironic twist, as it was only the third blue ribbon he had ever won in equitation. This victory, in one of the most prestigious classes of the season, had placed him out of novice equitation classes. Shortly thereafter, Brown qualified for the Maclay finals as well.

After Brown had qualified for the finals, Morris encouraged him to enter Sandsablaze in some schooling jumper classes in order to gain mileage over a more technical course. These classes would require a more demanding ride and pose some of the tests of accuracy that might be encountered at the finals. Often these jumper classes would be held at the end of a one-day show, making for an exceptionally long day for both horse and rider. On such occasions, the Browns would leave Derby Hill in the early hours of the morning and often would not be competing in the jumper ring until after dark.

At one such horse show, due to large numbers of competitors in the earlier events, Brown's jumper classes were not held until late in the evening. Sandsablaze was tacked up and waiting, only to encounter long delays as each competitor completed his rounds in the prior classes. Well after 10:00 p.m., the pair's class was finally called, and Brown and Sandsablaze were properly warmed up to enter the ring. Most of Brown's competitors in this class were professional jumper riders, including grand prix veteran Barney Ward and Olympic eventer Michael Page. These seasoned competitors were bored with the three-foot-six-inch jumps and decided to add a few rails to each of the standards. By the time Buddy and Sandsablaze were called to begin their round, the jumps were close to four feet in height.

Sandsablaze, refreshed from his nap, relished the added fence heights. He and Brown jumped the course well—so much so that Page called George Morris the following day to compliment him on the pair's performance. Brown was worried when he subsequently received a call from Morris, who asked if it were true that he was jumping Sandsablaze over four-foot fences. The teenager explained, best he could, that it was not his intent to jump so high; rather, he recalled, "It had just happened." To Brown's surprise, Morris was not angry but rather pleased. In Morris's eyes, this proved that Sandsablaze had the makings of a junior jumper.

CHAPTER 9
UPS AND DOWNS

Despite Brown's ambition and strong work ethic, the road to success in the junior jumpers was paved with difficulty for the teen and his horse. The junior jumper courses were higher than the pair was accustomed to and contained trappy fences and tighter distances. Sandsablaze also had a preference for solid footing and did not take kindly to mud or deep sand. Brown found this out firsthand in the spring of 1972 as the pair trained at Hunterdon in preparation for the spring shows. A deluge of spring rain had overrun the ring with mud, and the uneven footing and puddles were not to Sandsablaze's liking.

In addition to the undesirable footing, the tight, twisting turns of the jumper courses did not come naturally to the lanky Sandsablaze. As Brown had not yet learned how to properly balance the horse, the pair often struggled to remain on their feet while galloping around these winding turns. Sandsablaze would fall multiple times in the course of a lesson, with Brown typically landing alongside him in the mud. By lesson's end, the horse's white legs and face were streaked with mud, and Brown's rust-colored britches took on a sandy hue.

After such lessons, Sandsablaze would receive a thorough grooming, during which Buddy would curry and brush him to remove the caked-in dirt. Like many thin-skinned Thoroughbreds, Pappy did not care much for being curried, but he accepted it as a necessary task. After the horse was groomed and wrapped, Brown would clean himself up for the car ride home, picking tiny pieces of mud and dirt out of his own boots and dampened socks. At one point, after a particularly difficult lesson, Graham Brown asked his son if he wanted to give up and try something different. But the teenager wanted to keep on going; Sandsablaze was not about to give up, and neither was he.

In addition to staying on their feet, Brown and Pappy struggled with finding the correct takeoff distances to the trappy jumper-style fences that had become a central part of their lessons. Brown had difficulty adjusting his eye from a hunter way of riding a course to a more technical jumper style. One line of jumps, Brown recalls, was particularly difficult for the pair. This line consisted of a vertical fence with a short four strides leading up to a two-oxer combination with a twenty-six-foot distance. Brown would later tell the *Chronicle of the Horse*:

> *With my hunter eye, I'd find the slow long (distance) out of the corner to the vertical. Then it would be a slow four steps to the base of the first oxer, and then Sandsablaze would hurl his little body straight up to get away from the front rail and land slithering down the back rail. Then the next stride would be as big as he could make it, but we'd still be ten feet away from the base of the next oxer. He and I would hurl ourselves into the air like a flying squirrel, with his legs sprawled out reaching for the back rail. A lot of times he didn't get there. He and I would go tumbling into the dirt together. But Sandsablaze kept getting up like Rocky and saying, "OK, let's try again."*[5]

The pair made their season debut that year at the Boulder Brook horse show in Scarsdale, New York. It was a long day of showing for Brown, as many competitors had returned home from the winter shows in Florida and the classes were filled beyond capacity. The volume of competitors jumping two rounds apiece extended the show well into the evening, with Brown's classes not being called until close to eleven o'clock at night. The jumper classes were held indoors in a smallish arena, with firm, even footing that appeared to be to Sandsablaze's liking. The pair competed at this show in the preliminary jumper division over four-foot fences, earning a ribbon in their first class. By the time the second class was called, however, Sandsablaze was sound asleep in his tack. While warming him up, Brown had to use his leg and stick to get the horse properly "jazzed up" for jumping.

The conditions for the next class were challenging at best, as the lighting had dimmed substantially in the indoor, making it difficult to properly judge distances. As a result, Buddy recalls, he and Pappy "took a couple of headers in the indoor during warm-up," but once they had adjusted to the conditions, they performed well enough to earn another ribbon. Their next show, at Syracuse, had less than stellar results, as the pair fell at least two times while attempting some tight turns. "We still had a long way to go in mastering these turns and courses," Brown later said. "We were still very much a work in progress."

By the time of the fabled Devon Horse Show, Brown and Sandsablaze had improved steadily, completing more turns while staying upright and limiting their falls to once or twice per week. Brown had been looking forward to competing Sandsablaze successfully in the junior jumper division, but the late spring weather was uncooperative with this plan. A heavy rainstorm had dumped inches of rain on the show grounds, which left the famed Dixon Gold Ring teeming with puddles. The sand was drenched, rendering it deep and cuppy—the exact type of footing that caused Sandsablaze to struggle. As a result, Brown and Sandsablaze fell several times during their classes, reliving the mud-filled lessons they had experienced in the spring at Hunterdon.

The junior jumper division at the 1972 Devon Horse Show posed challenges for Buddy and Sandsablaze. *Photo courtesy of Buddy Brown.*

Brown recalls hearing the snide comments and whispers from onlookers who felt that the pair should simply give up. While many would have done just that due to frustration, embarrassment or fear, Brown and his trusted mount persevered. "The little guy kept getting up, and so did I," Brown later recalled. "I hadn't gotten hurt yet, and neither had he. I was young. At that age, I didn't know what I should worry about. Later in my career, I might not have kept getting up."[6]

In spite of such difficulties, the pair continued to work together. By the end of that summer, Brown and Sandsablaze were steadily improving as a team, remaining on their feet more often than not and earning some good ribbons in the junior jumper classes. The teen often talked to his horse while galloping in the arena, which gave Pappy an added sense of security with Brown in the saddle. Perhaps as a result of the challenges they had faced together, the bond between young Brown and Sandsablaze had become firmly cemented.

In late October, the pair headed to the Pennsylvania National Horse Show at Harrisburg for their first appearance in the coveted AHSA Medal finals. The Medal is the oldest national equitation final, having been founded in 1937 by Adrian Van Sinderen, then president of the AHSA. In its first

Buddy and Sandsablaze are shown here in the junior jumper division at Ox Ridge in 1972. *Photo courtesy of Buddy Brown.*

decade, the hunt seat medal final was contested in one session that also included the saddle seat and stock seat medals. In 1948, the three disciplines were separated into individual finals, with an award presented for each. The first winner of the AHSA hunt seat medal was Barbara Pease, who would later go on to start a successful line of Welsh ponies under the "Glenmore" name. Barbara Pease's name was engraved on the Adrian Van Sinderen Trophy; since that time, the name of every subsequent winner has been engraved on the coveted silver cup.

A win in the Medal finals is among the most prestigious of victories for a junior rider. Since its inception, the event has served as a precursor to success at the Olympic and grand prix levels. In fact, according to data from the United States Equestrian Foundation, approximately one-third of Medal finals champions have later joined Olympic and/or world championship teams. Indeed, the list of winners reads like a "who's who" of equestrian icons.

The Medal course is technical and demanding, with fences typically set at three feet, six inches and spreads extending as wide as five feet. Of the hundreds of riders competing at the finals in any one year, the top performers may be tested by the judges to further whittle down the pack. These tests could include trotting a jump, riding without stirrups, flatwork and any other tests that appeared in the AHSA rulebook. At the time in which Buddy and Sandsablaze competed, it was common for the judges to ask the top exhibitors to switch horses for the final testing phase. This would allow riders to demonstrate how they could handle an unfamiliar mount under pressure.

Brown arrived at the finals with few expectations, as equitation was a new endeavor for both the teen and his horse. Maintaining focus, the pair performed extremely well, making it all the way into the final testing phase from an original field of approximately 115 young riders. Brown and Sandsablaze, in their first showing at the finals, placed second behind fellow Hunterdon student—and future Olympian—Katie Monahan (now Prudent). This finish, which was well beyond Brown's expectations, proved that Sandsablaze truly had the makings of an equitation horse.

After Harrisburg, Brown and Sandsablaze traveled to New York City for the Maclay finals held at the National Horse Show. The inexperienced pair once again far exceeded expectations, placing third in elite competition. Future Olympian Leslie Burr (now Howard) won the finals, with Brown's friend Robin Rost placing second. It was a highly successful showing for Brown and Sandsablaze, who were still in the process of learning about balance and collection.

Around this time, Brown was given the opportunity to ride some of the nation's top show horses for Winter Place Farm in Salisbury, Maryland. The stable, owned by James Bradley Caine, was known for its magnificence and its ever-growing string of champion horses. The farm was adorned with chandeliers and water fountains, which surrounded an opulent barn that was home to some of the world's best horses and riders. It was Caine's intent to purchase the most successful animals in the nation, creating a showplace of champions that would dominate the equestrian circuit. This opportunity enabled Brown to gain experience aboard some of the nation's top hunters and jumpers. While at Winter Place,

Buddy and Sandsablaze accept a ribbon after the 1972 Maclay finals at the National Horse Show. *Photo courtesy of Buddy Brown.*

Brown competed in his first grand prix jumper class, ultimately placing seventh aboard the grey gelding L'arc en Ciel.

As Brown competed on the Florida circuit with Winter Place Farm, Sandsablaze was given some well-deserved time off at pasture. Graham Brown recalls observing Pappy as he relished this time spent "just being a horse," munching on hay and dried grass as his thick coat collected snowflakes. After enjoying the winter off from work, Sandsablaze would be well rested for the upcoming show season.

CHAPTER 10

RIDING TO THE TOP

The winter ushered in a new year, and the snow melted away, leaving spring in its wake. The new season brought with it an air of confidence for Brown and Pappy, and the troubles that had plagued them in previous seasons began to appear as a distant memory. Fresh from his time off from work, Sandsablaze trained well over fences and on the flat. In the prior season, he and Buddy had competed in the preliminary jumpers with some success. By the spring of 1973, they had worked their way up to the intermediate jumper division, competing over fences measuring up to four feet, six inches in height.

At Devon that year, the pair experienced a major breakthrough, posting a clear round in their first intermediate class to earn a berth in the jump-off along with three other horse-rider duos. Leading the pack was none other than Rodney Jenkins, who was riding a five-year-old black gelding by the name of Double Dice. Jenkins, who typically rode multiple horses in a single class, also qualified for the jump-off with a horse called Determined Dice. Both horses, the entries of noted horseman Harry Gill, had been named in homage to Jenkins's top mount, Gill's jumper Idle Dice.

Competing against the iconic Jenkins in Devon's famed Gold Ring, Brown's heart thumped excitedly as he trotted Sandsablaze into the arena. Brown and Pappy rose to this great challenge, clearing all the obstacles without error in a time of 37.79 seconds. They would be narrowly bested only by the veteran Jenkins aboard Double Dice, who clocked in slightly ahead of the pair at 37.67 seconds. Jenkins followed in third at 39.02 on his other mount, Determined

Dice, with Joy Slater and Space Citation finishing slightly behind in fourth. For the barely seventeen-year-old Buddy Brown aboard a horse deemed unlikely to jump above three feet, six inches, finishing second behind Jenkins was a truly amazing accomplishment. Jenkins himself was impressed by the young pair and offered accolades to Brown and Sandsablaze as they rode by. It was an incredible feeling for Brown when his longtime idol remarked, "We'll be seeing a lot of you in the jumper ring."

As Brown and Pappy continued to improve, Morris suggested that the pair attend a "screening trial" for the USET. These trials were held in the year after the Olympic Games in order to identify new talent for the team. As many of the USET riders were veterans gaining in years, the team was in search of some younger riders to prepare for the 1976 Olympics. In June 1973, Brown and Sandsablaze headed to the USET training headquarters in Gladstone, New Jersey, where they would "audition" before the team's legendary coach, Bertalan "Bert" de Némethy.

Born in 1911 in Hungary, de Némethy had served as a cavalry officer in his native country and, later, as a show jumper and instructor in Germany. After the cancellation of the 1940 Olympic Games, de Némethy was sent to train at the cavalry school in Hanover, where he learned the German method of training horses, which involved the use of cavaletti, gymnastics and principles of dressage. As the coach of the USET, he would successfully utilize all of these methods in schooling the U.S. horses with unanimously positive results.

The time spent working under de Némethy would prove invaluable for Brown and Sandsablaze. The jumping grids and gymnastics helped Sandsablaze to tighten up his front end over fences, and the dressage methods assisted Brown in better understanding how to collect the horse. It was, as Brown recalls, similar to being in college, with de Némethy utilizing classroom lectures to augment the lessons taught in the saddle. As de Némethy explained the biomechanics of equine movement, Brown and the other students were able to gain a better understanding of balance and collection. De Némethy also placed a strong emphasis on on-the-ground horsemanship, with hours devoted to cleaning tack and performing related barn chores.

After returning home to Derby Hill, Brown applied what he had learned at the screening trials in his daily schooling sessions with Pappy. Brown worked daily with Sandsablaze both in the saddle and on the ground, and the bond between horse and rider continued to strengthen. Brown's dedication to Sandsablaze led to increasing success in the show ring; in late June, the pair earned the coveted junior jumper championship at the Lake Placid Horse Show in New York.

Following this victory, the pair traveled to Cleveland, Ohio, to compete at the Chagrin Valley PHA Horse Show. There, Sandsablaze would be faced with a new challenge on the course—a wide water jump with a vertical rail. As Brown schooled the horse over the unfamiliar jump, Pappy slipped and fell, clipping a front leg on the wooden rail as he attempted to gain his balance. This mishap resulted in a skin laceration on Sandsablaze's leg, which would require several stitches. A subsequent veterinary examination revealed that the horse's tendon sheath had been bruised below the skin. Pappy would require six weeks off to recover, with much of that time spent on stall rest.

Sandsablaze was typically quiet in his stall, with one exception—feeding time. When it came time for grain, one had to be very careful about entering the horse's stall. "He was like a raptor at feeding time," Buddy Brown remembers. "Ears pinned, teeth bared, you name it." Feeding the horse could be a challenge, particularly if his feed bucket were not situated close enough to the door. "He would kick out as a warning if he felt his grain was not being delivered in a timely manner," said Brown. The horse was otherwise a perfect gentleman, not only in his stall but also while being led or handled.

As Sandsablaze recovered at Derby Hill, the bond between horse and rider grew stronger. Brown tended to the horse's daily treatments, which involved running cold water down the injured leg, icing the tendon, applying a poultice to draw out swelling and wrapping both front legs in bandages for support. While Sandsablaze was most certainly not a cuddly pet, he appeared to relish every moment spent with his young master. Likewise, Brown's efforts to bond with Sandsablaze on the ground seemed to enhance the connection between horse and rider in the saddle.

With time and determination on the part of Brown, Sandsablaze's injury responded well to treatment. In late summer, the horse's veterinarian determined that Pappy was ready to resume training. Brown slowly brought the horse back into work, ensuring that Sandsablaze did not over-exert himself during this rehabilitation period. By the time the first signs of autumn arrived and the trees began to change color, Sandsablaze was back in show ring form. While the pair's preparation time had been shortened by several weeks, Brown would be able to ride Sandsablaze at the upcoming equitation finals.

The 1973 AHSA Medal Finals were larger than ever, drawing close to 120 competitors. In preparation for this level of competition, Sandsablaze was given a slight change of tack. While Sandsablaze was typically ridden in a snaffle, his bit was changed to a Pelham for the finals, as the curb rein allowed Brown to collect the horse a bit more easily. Brown remembers that it was almost impossible to get Sandsablaze into a frame at this point, and the teenager did not understand enough about the process of obtaining a proper connection. The ewe-necked Sandsablaze would travel with his neck "upside down and hollow" as Brown attempted, often unsuccessfully, to wriggle it down via contact with the reins.

Bedecked in his new bit and a standing martingale, Sandsablaze performed exceptionally well over several rounds, with Brown remaining calm and poised in the face of added pressure. When the teen was called back in the final group for additional testing, Brown was required to swap horses with fellow competitor Nancy Baroody. Brown gained the ride on the champion hunter War Dress, while Baroody was chosen to ride Sandsablaze around the course for the final phase of the competition. Sandsablaze was a willing mount for Baroody; however, the horse's deceivingly long stride ultimately worked in Brown's favor, as it was difficult for other riders to estimate the number of strides required between fences. As Baroody guided Sandsablaze around the course, the horse left out a stride in a bending line—an error that moved Brown into the top spot overall. Brown later told the *Chronicle of the Horse*, "I won't say I looked as pretty as Nancy, but between my riding and (Pappy's) help, we won."[7] Brown's name was engraved on the Adrian Van Sinderen Trophy, where it stood among those of the many legends who had preceded him in this win.

Prior to the final testing, a horse show photographer had snapped a photo of Brown and Sandsablaze as they made their way around the course. That photograph has since become iconic in the sport, having appeared in George Morris's later printings of *Hunter Seat Equitation*. Morris used this photo as an example of excellence for other hunter seat riders to follow. "Buddy Brown and his legendary Sandsablaze are showing us all how easily it can be done with the proper mental attitude," Morris wrote in his book. "Both are doing their job perfectly, yet without a trace of stiffness."

Bolstered by their win at Harrisburg, Brown and Sandsablaze headed to the National Horse Show as favorites to win the Maclay finals. Brown hoped to join the small and elite group of riders who had garnered victory in both the Medal and the Maclay. After several successful rounds, the pair was once again called back in the final group for a ride-off. This test, to be ridden without stirrups, involved jumping an oxer from the corner of the ring and, upon landing, trotting to the next fence, an upright vertical. As the pair

This photo of Buddy and Sandsablaze winning the 1973 AHSA Medal finals became famous after appearing in George Morris's book *Hunter Seat Equitation*. *Reprinted with permission of the* Chronicle of the Horse.

approached the oxer, Brown gave Pappy extra pressure from his leg to ensure that the horse would clear the spooky-looking fence. However, the added aids gave Sandsablaze some extra impulsion on the landing, rendering it virtually impossible for Brown to bring him back to the trot. As a result, Sandsablaze produced, as Brown recalls, "eight of the tiniest little canter strides you have ever seen."

Those canter steps were not lost on the eyes of the judges, nor on the many spectators who had gathered excitedly in the stands. A hush came over the crowd, followed by a chorus of chatters, as the audience became aware of the young rider's mistake. Due to the heightened competition in the class, that one error pushed Brown and Sandsablaze out of the top standings. Disappointed in his own misjudgment, Brown gave the gallant horse an extra pat on the neck for his efforts. At the age of seventeen, Brown would be eligible for one last attempt at winning the Maclay finals the following year.

By this time, Buddy and Pappy had amassed a local fan following. Bill Rube, now co-chair of the U.S. Hunter Jumper Association (USHJA) Wheeler Museum Committee and a two-time winner of the USHJA's Distinguished Service Award, remembers his days as a young teenager spent at various East Coast horse shows. Rube recalls planting himself at ringside, hugging the rail, in order to gain a glimpse of the pair as they made their way around the course.

"Buddy and Sandsablaze were the ones to watch," Rube recalls. "Hunters, equitation and jumpers—they did it all." Rube remembers one attribute in particular that made Brown stand out: he always seemed genuinely happy to be sitting atop that bright chestnut horse. "It did not matter if he had a good or a bad round," Rube says. "He always made sure to smile and give Pappy a pat on the neck for his efforts. There was an amazing connection between Buddy and that horse, and it was simply a pleasure to watch."

CHAPTER 11

OFF TO EUROPE

In the early part of 1974, seventeen-year-old Buddy Brown was chosen to represent the United States in Europe as a member of the USET on its grand prix tour. This trip, which would last from June through August, would take Brown and Sandsablaze to West Germany, France, the UK and Ireland. The purpose of the tour, according to an account in the *New York Times*, was to give "some young riders and inexperienced horses a look at some stiff international competition."[8]

Joining Brown on the tour were three other young riders: Robert Ridland of California, Michael Matz from Pennsylvania and Dennis Murphy, the son of an Alabama sharecropper. Of the four riders, only the twenty-three-year-old Ridland had experience competing overseas, as he had been a part of the USET at the 1972 Olympics in Munich. Veteran Olympian Frank Chapot would join mid-tour in France, adding some valuable skill to the team of up-and-coming riders. Rodney Jenkins would also be joining the team at a later date in England, where he would ride the legendary Idle Dice and Number One Spy. Interestingly, while Jenkins was a seasoned veteran in U.S. competition, he had yet to compete in a European grand prix.

The term *grand prix* may be translated from French into the words "greatest prize." It is no wonder, then, that grand prix show jumping is the pinnacle of equestrian jumping sports. A grand prix jumper competes over a twisting, technical course where jumps might reach five feet, three inches in height and spreads might extend to six feet, seven inches. The element of speed is added in the jump-off round, where riders aim to complete the course with the fewest penalties in the fastest time.

In the late spring of 1974, Brown and Sandsablaze reported to the USET training center in Gladstone for several weeks of rigorous schooling under Coach Bert de Némethy. There, they were joined by teammates Ridland, Murphy and Matz, along with their various horses. In addition to Sandsablaze, Buddy would bring along two grey geldings for the tour: Aries and A Little Bit. The latter, a Thoroughbred recently off the track, was a promising young jumper who was, in fact, still eligible for the first-year green hunter division. Graham Brown had purchased A Little Bit (registered under the name Grey Crossing) as a prospect only months before, and the horse had impressed Morris and de Némethy during previous training sessions. A Little Bit and Aries would be used for individual speed classes, while Brown chose the more consistent Sandsablaze for team events.

Other horses joining on the tour of Europe included Snow Flurry, Mighty Ruler and Post Time, all of which would be ridden by Buddy's teammate Michael Matz. Dennis Murphy would bring along four mounts for the

The grey gelding A Little Bit was another of Buddy's mounts during the 1974 European tour. *Photo courtesy of Buddy Brown.*

occasion—Do Right, Tuscaloosa, Triple Crown and Flying John—while Ridland would ride Almost Persuaded, Balalaika and Boy Colonel. Ridland would also gain the ride on Main Spring for the early part of the tour until Chapot arrived to take over the reins when the competition reached La Baule, France.

James "Jimmy" Herring, who worked at that time as a groom for Michael Matz, remembers Sandsablaze well. While Herring admired and trusted Bert de Némethy's judgment, he admits to feeling somewhat befuddled when he first saw Sandsablaze in his stall at Gladstone. "My first thought," Herring recalls, "was that I wondered what Bert was thinking. We were heading toward a grand prix tour, and this was an equitation horse." Herring's reaction serves to illustrate the unusual feat that Sandsablaze would accomplish; it was virtually unheard of for an equitation mount to graduate into Olympic-level competition. Once Herring saw Sandsablaze in action, however, he realized the horse was right where he belonged.

Late in the afternoon on May 28, 1974, the USET horses and riders, along with all of the necessary tack and equipment for a months-long overseas stay, were loaded onto a plane at Kennedy Airport. Sandsablaze and the other horses were groomed to perfection, their legs were carefully bandaged and they were loaded onto the waiting airplane. All of the animals were loaded without trouble, and last-minute instructions were given to the grooms and riders. In the book *The U.S. Equestrian Team Book of Riding* by the legendary William Steinkraus, team member Dennis Murphy recalled, "It was a tremendous feeling when the plane finally left the ground and we knew we were on our way. Bert de Némethy and some of the grooms knew what to expect, but for most of us, we were heading to the great unknown."[9]

The flight landed in Frankfurt, Germany, in the early hours of the following day. The team was given a warm welcome upon entering this foreign land, and Sandsablaze and the other horses settled in well. Preparations were made for the team's show debut, which was to occur at Germany's International Horse Show at Wiesbaden, a city in the Frankfurt Rhine Main Region, during the first week of June. "We hope to give a good account of ourselves," Bert de Némethy told the media in his trademark Hungarian accent. "But the main aim is to give our young riders and horses international experience."[10]

Upon arriving at the show grounds, Brown was able to catch a glimpse of the Wiesbaden course, where he and Sandsablaze would compete in their first-ever grand prix. In addition to the newness of this level of competition for the pair, the sheer height and width of the jumps was intimidating for

Brown. The European courses were much more solid than those back home in the United States; the turf was dotted with permanent obstacles, such as banks, ditches and water hazards, which required a bold, forward ride. Additionally, the events in Europe typically included three grueling rounds rather than two, which were designed to test the stamina of the world's best horses and riders. In the final round—the jump-off—the rails were typically raised higher.

Having never jumped Sandsablaze over such a daunting course, Brown began to have second thoughts as to whether the pair would be up for the challenge. Pappy had never competed at the grand prix level, and Brown wondered whether the horse was athletic enough to clear these solid jumps. Brown brought his concerns to de Némethy, who suggested that it was time for the pair to rise to this new challenge.

Brown gathered his courage and patted Sandsablaze's strong, silky neck as the pair entered the ring for the first round of competition. The teenager looked around at the stands that surrounded the arena, which were filled to capacity with cheering, waving German fans. Taking a deep breath, Brown began his opening circle, asking Pappy for several changes of lead in order to rev him up for the challenge to come. (This exercise, developed by Coach de Némethy, became Sandsablaze's signature entrance into the ring.) To Brown's surprise, the little horse rallied around the course of solid fences, clearing each and every obstacle without a single fault. Pappy repeated this flawless performance in the second round, which earned the pair a berth in the jump-off alongside some of the world's most decorated horses and riders.

Brown's eyes widened as he watched the show officials raise the fences for the jump-off. The obstacles appeared almost monumental as their shiny rails cast shadows in the sun. As Brown urged Sandsablaze into a gallop, the teenager's eyes caught sight of the final jump on the course—a huge oxer measuring five feet, three inches high and six feet wide, which was constructed of eight or nine heavy white rails that surrounded a hedge. The shrubbery itself was over four feet tall and nearly just as wide. While cantering by this particularly daunting obstacle, Brown recalled that the height of the fence reached as high as his waist while mounted.

Swallowing his fear, Brown put all his faith in Sandsablaze, who tackled each jump without fault as the pair's teammates watched from the sidelines. Brown kept his composure until he approached that last, enormous oxer, when his self-preservation instincts appeared to take over. Sitting back in the saddle, which caused him to lift his hands, Brown urged Sandsablaze

The fences in Europe were much larger and more solid than those in the United States. *Photo courtesy of the USET Foundation.*

forward with his legs to cue the horse over the monstrous fence. "My eyes were as big as saucers," Brown remembered, "and I am sure his were, too. I was looking over the back rail of this jump, thinking, 'There is no way.' Then, all of the sudden, I felt him start tucking up underneath me. I will remember this as long as I have a memory. He brought his wither and back up and brought his right lead up in front of him like I had never felt before. This was what the training was all about—how to keep the outside hind under control."[11]

In an instant, Brown recalls, every lesson he had learned from Morris and de Némethy came surging together. As the teen held his breath and closed his eyes, Sandsablaze rose up and boldly cleared the fence. At that moment, Brown recalls, the pair had reached a new level, with a performance good enough to place fourth overall. As the white satin rosette was affixed to Sandsablaze's leather bridle, Brown felt an enormous sense of pride in his equine partner.

While Brown celebrated his first ribbon-winning performance of the tour, the Europeans—who were accustomed to huge horses with scope

Despite being intimidated by the size of the fences, Buddy and Sandsablaze performed well enough to earn a ribbon in Germany. *Photo courtesy of the USET Foundation.*

Buddy and Sandsablaze are shown in a candid photo during the parade for ribbons at Wiesbaden. *Photo courtesy of Buddy Brown.*

and bascule—were not quite sure what to make of Sandsablaze and his unique style. The little Thoroughbred would often "feel his way" around a course, rubbing every jump as if to measure its height using his legs. As Sandsablaze's white legs skimmed along the top rails, the "clunk-clunk" against each obstacle was readily audible to ringside spectators. Those rubs aside, Sandsablaze jumped consistently clean more often than not and, according to Brown, never refused fences.

Brown's teammate Michael Matz remembers the heart and honesty that Sandsablaze showed to his rider. Matz recalls that "Sandsablaze was a very quiet horse. He was not the scopiest horse, but he tried as hard as he could. Both he and Buddy were inexperienced at the grand prix level, and they helped each other. Sandsablaze gave Buddy everything he had—even more than one would expect of his ability."

Following the grand prix at Wiesbaden, the team traveled to Lucerne, Switzerland, where it would compete in its first Nations Cup class. From the perspective of an international team, the Nations Cup is the most crucial event of a show. Nations Cup courses are typically longer than other classes and have a tighter time limit than individual events. These classes, where countries compete against one another, consist of two rounds, with a third timed round added in the event of a tie. A country may enter up to four riders in the class, with the three best scores counting toward each team's total.

Brown was nervous entering his first Nations Cup, as he hoped to perform well enough to boost his team in the standings. Despite a few baubles, the rookie team performed reasonably well, placing fourth overall behind Great Britain, West Germany and Switzerland in tight competition. Brown cheered as teammate Robert Ridland won the Grand Prix of Lucerne aboard the bay mare Almost Persuaded and later partnered with Ridland for a win in the relay event. All in all, it was a positive experience for the young U.S. team.

After Lucerne, the team headed to La Baule, France, where it would compete in another Nations Cup class. As there was a slight break in between shows, the team opted to take its horses on a short hack to a nearby beach. While the other horses bathed their legs in the cool salt water, Sandsablaze required some coaxing from the grooms in order to place his feet in the surf. Once he had entered the water, however, Pappy appeared to thoroughly enjoy it, splashing and playfully tossing his head as he attempted to lie down and roll in the ocean. In fact, as Brown would later discover, this experience might have made Sandsablaze a bit too comfortable with water; after his day at the beach, the horse appeared to misunderstand that water is an element to be jumped over—rather than galloped through—on course. Thereafter, Sandsablaze often put a foot in the water when faced with such a jump on course.

Refreshed from their time on the beach, Sandsablaze and the others prepared for the horse show at La Baule in France, where the team was joined by veteran Frank Chapot. Bolstered by Chapot's experience and a near-clean round from Buddy and Sandsablaze, the United States placed a game second behind West Germany in the Nations Cup. As Sandsablaze's only faults occurred when he placed a foot in the water, Coach de Némethy suggested additional schooling over the water jump in preparation for the upcoming shows. Brown and Sandsablaze practiced over the water-filled ditch in the wee hours of the morning. A rail was added to the jump to help the horse understand that the water was meant to be jumped rather than cantered through. When Sandsablaze cleared the water jump in an unorthodox fashion during these practices, the twisting of his body often sent Brown flying across the dewy grass. The end result of the practice was successful, although de Némethy continued to routinely school Brown and Sandsablaze over water jumps to ensure that the horse retained this lesson.

After La Baule, it was on to England, where the USET would compete on the world-famous Hickstead course. Rodney Jenkins would join the team for this show, which was also the site of the world championships. The show was managed by Douglas "Dougie" Bunn, who had created the All England Jumping Course at Hickstead in Sussex in 1960. Bunn's course, known as one of the toughest in the world, included a series of daunting obstacles such as the "Devil's Dyke"—three fences in short succession with a water-filled ditch in the middle—and the Derby Bank, a drop jump characterized by a ten-foot slope down the front.

Overall, the Hickstead show was a success, with Chapot and Jenkins competing in the prestigious world championship finals. In this event, the top four riders were required to switch horses—a test of skill that was reminiscent of the equitation finals, albeit over much higher fences. Brown and the other members of the USET applauded as Chapot finished a respectable third overall behind the eventual champion, Hartwig Steenken of West Germany. Among his other accomplishments, Steenken had won a team gold medal at the 1972 Olympic Games, placing fourth overall in the individual Olympic jumping final.

After Hickstead, the USET moved on to Wembley in London, England, where Brown and Sandsablaze competed in yet another Nations Cup event.

Buddy and Sandsablaze faced some of the largest fences they had ever seen during their 1974 tour of Europe. *Photo courtesy of the USET Foundation.*

Driven by a clear round from Brown and the little chestnut gelding, the USET finished as runner-up behind the home team of Great Britain. It was an impressive showing overall for the U.S. team, with several members winning additional classes. In the John Player Grand Prix, the highlight of the Wembley show, Brown and Sandsablaze posted multiple clear rounds to once again earn a place in the jump-off. The pair finished their final round in a respectable 40.5 seconds, which was good enough to earn a third-place ribbon behind teammate Jenkins and legendary British rider David Broome. Following Wembley, the competition continued in Cardiff, Wales, where Buddy was proud to finish second behind Rodney Jenkins in a thrilling ride-off between the amateur and professional competitors. The final stop on the tour would be Dublin, the site of the famed Grand Prix of Ireland.

CHAPTER 12
LUCK OF THE IRISH

The Dublin Horse Show has a rich and storied history that dates back to 1864. In that inaugural show, hosted by the Royal Agricultural Society of Ireland, an estimated 366 entries competed for prize money totaling £520. By 1868, the show featured "leaping" (or "lepping") demonstrations, in which horses were ridden over various—and often daunting—obstacles. That year, Richard Flynn and his hunter, Shane Rhue, won the Stone Wall competition, "clearing an obstacle of progressive height ultimately measuring six feet," according to the Dublin Horse Show's website. Interestingly, Shane Rhue was sold for £1,000 later that same day.[12]

In 1870, the show was renamed the National Horse Show and was combined with Ireland's Annual Sheep Show. By this time, the horse lepping events included, in addition to the stone wall, "a wide leap over 2½ foot gorse-filled hurdle with 12 feet of water on the far side." The original rules of the competition stated simply that "the obstacles had to be cleared to the satisfaction of the judges." The first continuous lepping course was introduced in 1881; by that time, the show had become popular enough to warrant a viewing stand to accommodate eight hundred spectators.

The idea of hosting an international jumping competition was first suggested by Jakob Ziegler, a colonel in the Swiss army, in 1925. At the time, the Aga Khan, upon hearing of such an event, offered a challenge trophy to be presented to the winner of the event. The following year, international competitions were introduced at the Dublin Horse Show, and the inaugural Nations Cup for the Aga Khan Challenge trophy was held. Competing for the original Aga Khan Challenge Trophy in 1926 were Ireland, Great Britain, Holland, Belgium, France and Switzerland, with the latter capturing the coveted trophy on Irish-bred horses. All riders were military officers, as nonmilitary riders would not be allowed to compete in the Nations Cup until 1949. (British rider Peter Robeson would be the first civilian to compete in the Nations Cup. Riding a horse called Craven A, Robeson helped his team capture the Nations Cup that year.)

The year 1934 saw the introduction of the first grand prix, whose winner receives the coveted "Irish Trophy." The inaugural winner was Commandant J.D. (Jed) O'Dwyer of the Army Equitation school. By 1974, the grand prix had become one of the most prestigious events of the international circuit, attracting the top competitors from various countries. Buddy and Sandsablaze would face competitors from a deep well of talent that included, among others, the reigning world champion and Olympic gold medalist, Hartwig Steenken of West Germany, and former world champion and Olympic medalist David Broome of the UK.

Prior to the grand prix, the jumper events opened with a series of different classes, one of which was the BP Chase held on August 8. Despite their inexperience, Brown and Sandsablaze were up to the task, posting double clear rounds to qualify for the jump-off. Also entered in the jump-off were five other horse-rider duos, including Brown's teammate and friend, Michael Matz aboard Mighty Ruler. First to tackle the twisting course was Nelson Pessoa of Brazil, whose horse, Pernod, struggled over a few of the fences, accumulating twelve faults in 72.9 seconds. Next to jump were New Zealand's John Cottle and Fritz Ligges of West Germany; each dropped two rails for a total of eight faults. Matz and Mighty Ruler fared much better, completing the course with just four faults in 73.2 seconds.

On the heels of Matz's positive ride, Brown gathered Sandsablaze and galloped into the ring. Not only did Sandsablaze jump the course clean, but the pair also shaved seconds off Matz's posted time. Still to take to the course, however, was the veteran David Broome of England, who earned cheers from the crowd as he entered the arena aboard the solid bay gelding Sportsman. As expected, Broome galloped smoothly around the twisting course and appeared a clear winner with just one fence remaining. The crowd gasped in disbelief as Sportsman's hind leg grazed the last element, sending the white rail tumbling to the ground with a thud. When the scores were tallied, Brown—the unknown American teenager—had bested the venerable David Broome. The Irish media, reeling from the surprising turn of events, quipped, "Buddy Brown had luck on his side."[13]

Buddy and Sandsablaze clear a fence in their winning round in the BP Chase at the 1974 Dublin Horse Show. *Photo courtesy of the RDS Archives.*

Buddy and Sandsablaze (far right) with USET teammates Rodney Jenkins, Dennis Murphy and Michael Matz at the 1974 Dublin Horse Show. *Photo courtesy of the RDS Archives.*

Four days later, on August 12, Brown and Sandsablaze proved that their victory was anything but a fluke. The pair battled twenty other horse-rider combinations in the show's marquis event, the Grand Prix of Ireland, where they hoped to earn the £2,300 prize and a place among show jumping's elite. The class was much larger than the Nations Cup events, as there was no limit on how many entries were allowed from each country. Walking the course with Coach de Némethy, Brown expressed a newfound sense of confidence. "As we walked around the course," de Némethy later told the media, "we could see that it was quite a big one. I told (Buddy) that we could pull up if he wanted to. Buddy looked me right in the eye and said, 'I would like to win.' He (was) very determined to win, but his absolute determination comes in a very pleasant way."[14]

Brown's confident demeanor translated to a positive trip in the show ring. In the opening round of competition, Brown and Sandsablaze went clear, with only two other riders—Broome and his British teammate Peter Robeson—equaling this feat. The British team, fresh off a victory in the Aga Khan Trophy class, appeared poised for another win. In the second round, however, Broome's mount, Sportsman, clipped a rail on the fifth jump, while both Brown and Robeson posted clear rounds.

It now came down to a thrilling jump-off between Brown and the veteran Robeson, who, at the age of forty-five, was more than twice as old as the American teenager. Robeson entered the stadium first, riding clear until the problematic fence five caught him in its grips. Robeson and his mount, Grebe, the heroes of the Aga Khan Trophy class held days before, caught the back top part of the fence, knocking the heavy wooden rail to the ground. It was the only mistake made by the pair, who finished the course with four faults in a time of 53.1 seconds.

The massive Irish crowd was packed excitedly in the stands with not an empty seat visible to the naked eye. Voices were hushed as Brown and Sandsablaze entered the show ring in their typical calm and low-key fashion. Brown tossed his nerves aside at the in-gate, skillfully guiding Sandsablaze into the ring and past the massive crowds that lined the stadium. All the years of preparation came flooding into the teenager's mind. This was the young pair's moment to shine.

As the starting buzzer sounded and Sandsablaze began his opening gallop, Brown focused on the task ahead. While Sandsablaze touched a few rails with his characteristic clunking sound, not one rail slipped from its base. As the pair crossed the finish with a clear round in 53.3 seconds, the crowd erupted in admiration for the American teen and his trusted horse. The

Buddy and Sandsablaze enter the ring for their round in the Dublin Grand Prix in 1974. *Photo courtesy of the RDS Archives.*

media, now becoming somewhat familiar with this order of finish, noted, "Riding with strength and courage, Buddy Brown coaxed another clear round out of Sandsablaze."

The final placings read like a yearbook of show jumping royalty, with Robeson in second, Broome in third and Rodney Jenkins and Idle Dice in fourth based on a half-fault time penalty. Rounding out the final placings was a five-way tie between the great Harvey Smith aboard Salvador, Michael Matz and Mighty Ruler, world champion Hartwig Steenken and Kosmos, Alwin Schoeckemole and Rex the Robber and Commandant Raimondo d'Inzeo of Italy aboard Bellevere.

On the world's stage, Brown and Sandsablaze had triumphed, winning their first grand prix event. As of this writing, Brown remains the youngest rider to win the Grand Prix of Ireland. The humble pair led the victory gallop around the stadium as the joyful crowd erupted in a symphony of cheers. Sandsablaze stood quietly as the blue ribbon was affixed to his bridle, holding his large ears at attention as his teenaged master accepted the coveted silver trophy.

Sandsablaze relished the added attention that came with winning a major grand prix. Brown recalls that the little horse loved playing to the crowds

Above: Buddy and Sandsablaze dazzled the huge crowds at the 1974 Grand Prix of Ireland at the Dublin Horse Show. *Photo courtesy of the RDS Archives*.

Right: Sandsablaze is presented with a blue ribbon after winning the 1974 Grand Prix of Ireland. *Photo courtesy of the RDS Archives*.

Buddy and Sandsablaze lead the victory procession after winning the Grand Prix of Ireland in 1974. *Photo courtesy of the RDS Archives.*

and often acted as a "ham" for the cameras when his photograph was taken. Brown notes that Pappy was never spooky when approached by strangers; while other horses often leaped and shied during ribbon or medal ceremonies, Sandsablaze puffed himself up for the crowds with the confidence and style of an equine movie star.

Meanwhile, the victory had elevated Buddy Brown to celebrity status, as show jumping riders in Europe are revered like actors or rock stars. After the show, Brown's parents were approached by a young Irish boy, who asked Pattie for her autograph and requested that she "sign it like Buddy would." Later, as Brown and his teammates walked down the streets of Dublin, they were chased by a mob of teen girls who sought to grab a piece of the young rider's clothes or a lock of his thick, wavy, dark hair. On that day in Ireland, Brown and Sandsablaze had become bona fide celebrities.

CHAPTER 13
BACK IN THE STATES

After returning home to the United States in mid-August, Brown and Sandsablaze had some time to refresh before beginning the indoor competitions at home. That fall, the pair was selected to compete in the Nations Cup events at the Washington International Horse Show (WIHS) at the D.C. Armory in Washington, D.C. There, Brown would be reunited with two of his teammates from the European tour: Dennis Murphy on Do Right and Rodney Jenkins on Number One Spy. Joining this group for the indoor circuit were Thom Hardy and his horse, Coming Attraction. Hardy, like Brown and Murphy, was in his first year of international competition.

Established in 1958, the WIHS was, and remains, one of the most prestigious horse shows and part of the fall indoor circuit. According to the horse show's website, the show is "a place for professionals to make their marks, amateurs to get their start, the famous to socialize and kids to watch in awe."[15] The horse show was frequented by celebrities and politicians, including various U.S. presidents and first ladies through the years. The indoor shows in the early 1970s were known for their glamour and glitz; it was not uncommon for spectators to be dressed in furs and black ties as they watched their favorite horses and riders compete for the thrill of the sport.

The event at WIHS would mark Brown's first Nations Cup competition at home in the United States. While most countries were allowed to host one Nations Cup event, the United States, due to its larger size, was allotted two events per year—these were held at WIHS and at the National Horse Show in New York. The WIHS Nations Cup event in 1974 proved to be a relative cakewalk for the U.S. team, as all horses and riders performed flawlessly. Their win over France garnered the attention of various media, including the venerable *Sports Illustrated*, which wrote, "Here is an undeniable first. A United States Equestrian Team made up of rookies won the Nations Cup. (They) are pretty clearly shaping up as the best international jumping team on this continent."[16]

Following their success at Washington, Buddy and Sandsablaze competed as part of the Nations Cup team at the National Horse Show, which began on November 6 at Madison Square Garden. While Brown, by age, was technically still eligible to compete in the Maclay finals, he was unable to do so as a current member of the USET. Instead, Brown would be representing his country as a member of the Nations Cup team, competing not against other teens but rather against veteran riders and horses from all around the world.

The show jumping events in New York began with style and majesty, orchestrated with the usual flair that characterized the National Horse Show. In the opening ceremony, the Nations Cup teams were led into the arena by the Twenty-sixth Army Band of Fort Hamilton, whose riders were bedecked in double-breasted, gold-buttoned, navy blue uniforms. Lieutenant General James G. Kalergie, commander of the First Army, led the procession of international teams into the arena, with Sandsablaze trotting proudly behind him as a member of the USET. In an interesting turn of events, France was absent from the opening ceremony, as the team's interpreter had misunderstood the timing of the procession.

Joining Brown and Sandsablaze on the U.S. team were Dennis Murphy on Tuscaloosa, Thom Hardy on Coming Attraction and USET captain Frank Chapot on the grey Thoroughbred Good Twist. The international events began with the Cavcote Welcome Challenge Trophy in the afternoon, a class in which nineteen horse-rider combinations competed over a course of ten fences. The majority of horses and riders rose to the early challenge; of the original nineteen starters, fourteen posted clear rounds. Racing against the clock in the jump-off, Brown's teammate Dennis Murphy completed the course in 34.8 seconds, only to be bested for the top prize by the final rider on course, David Broome of Great Britain aboard Ballywillwill. Despite ultimately losing this class, the U.S. riders earned ten points toward the overall team championship, in which points are accumulated over a series of events.

In the evening, the riders convened over a more difficult course in a battle for the coveted Democrat Memorial Challenge Trophy (Democrat Trophy), the highlight of the day's events. The trophy had been named in honor of the brown Thoroughbred gelding Democrat, a legendary U.S. show jumper from the 1940s and 1950s. During his lengthy career, Democrat represented the United States on two Olympic teams and won numerous show jumping honors with both army and civilian riders.

With Brown and Sandsablaze in the mix, seventeen horse-rider teams were poised to compete over a course of eleven obstacles in front of the fashionable New York crowd. Buddy and Pappy galloped confidently into the ring, where Sandsablaze's white markings gleamed under the bright lights of Madison Square Garden. As the well-dressed crowd watched from the stands, the pair galloped cleanly over the course of eleven jumps in a blistering time of 31.6 seconds. Also posting clear rounds were France's Hubert Parot aboard Port Royal and Edward Campion, a commander from the Irish Equitation School, riding Garraieoin. However, neither Parot nor Campion, who completed the course in 34.7 and 38.9 seconds, respectively, could beat the time set by Brown and Sandsablaze. The young pair had just added another key win to their widely expanding résumé.

After being presented with the Democrat Trophy, a beaming Buddy Brown told the press, "Sandsablaze is a nice horse; he fools a lot of people. He rubs his fences, and ringsiders who do not know him think he's just about getting over. But I've been riding him for four years, and I don't worry when he rattles rails. He doesn't do more than he has to, but he gets the job done."[17] At eighteen years of age, Buddy was not only the youngest winner of the Democrat Trophy but also the youngest of all international show jumping competitors at the National Horse Show.

Brown's victory in the Democrat Trophy class propelled the USET well above the competing teams, as the United States finished with twenty points for the day's events—eight points ahead of Britain, its closest competitor. The following day, the *New York Times* reported, "The USET, which swept to victory in Washington last week, served notice yesterday to the rest of the international teams at the National Horse Show, which opened an eight-day run, that it was going to be hard to defeat."[18]

Over the course of the New York show, the U.S. team wrapped up the Nations Cup events, fueled by another flawless performance by Brown and Sandsablaze on November 11. In a series of two rounds spanning the afternoon and evening hours, the pair cleared sixteen fences without a single error. In the opening round, Brown and Sandsablaze took to the course first, setting the proverbial bar high as they cleared fence after fence without a fault. Murphy on Do Right and Thom Hardy on Coming Attraction followed, each posting additional clear rounds for the team and securing the top spot on the leader board with three teams left to compete.

While the USET made the course appear effortless, the remaining competitors—France, Britain and Canada—were not as fortunate. France experienced a difficult opening round, as its first horse-rider pair, Parot and Port Royal, grabbed two rails and accumulated nine and a half faults with a time penalty to boot. Fortunately, the team's next two entries were able to avenge Parot's performance, with Michael Roche aboard Un Espoir and Pierre Durand on Varin each posting clear rounds. The pressure mounted on the shoulders of the final French rider, women's world champion Jannou Tissote, when she began her opening circle aboard the gelding Rocket. As the crowd collectively held its breath, Tissote rose to the lofty challenge, piloting Rocket to a clear round. This performance kept Tissote's team in contention, as, under the Nations Cup rules, France was able to omit Parot's score from the total.

In contrast to France, Britain began the afternoon on a high note as its first two entries, Graham Fletcher on Tauna Dora and John Greenwood on Mr. Punch, posted clear rounds. Trouble ensued, however, when Peter Robeson aboard Grebe ran into difficulty, posting five faults. The pressure was now on David Broome to ride clean and keep the British team in contention. Broome, displaying the poise and control that had made him an international champion, reached into his deep well of experience and did just that.

Canada was the last team to qualify for the final, and it did so when three of its riders—Kelly Hall-Holland, Ian Miller and John Simpson—posted clear rounds. This set up for an exciting round of competition between the United States, France, Britain and Canada later that evening, as the stands were packed to capacity with fans who hoped for a thrilling duel to the finish. According to the *New York Times*, however, the second round was "a bit of an anticlimax" as Brown, Hardy and Murphy "breezed through easily for the U.S." With the three clear rounds counting toward the final score, the veteran Chapot was able to sit out this event and rest his horse for future competition.

The British team performed fairly well but was unable to match the challenge posed by the United States. Canada was out of contention early in the round, owing to a barrage of faults posted in succession by Hall-Holland, John Bannister and Simpson; Miller was the only Canadian to post a clear second round.

When France took to the ring as the final team remaining, it provided some much-needed excitement. Both Parot and Roche posted clear rounds, setting the stage for a clean performance by one of the team's last two riders. A rail down by Varin and a refusal by Rocket put this possibility to rest, ensuring yet another victory for the USET. Anchored by Brown and Sandsablaze, the home team had accumulated a whopping seventy-six final points, twenty points more than Britain and well above the totals posted by France and Canada.

Following this victory, Chapot told the media, "Winning with this rider roster has to make everyone happy. Thom has been in only two international horse shows and he's been on two winning Nations Cup teams. Dennis came off of a farm, outside Tuscaloosa, to ride with us in Europe this summer. Until then he'd never seen a Nations Cup, much less ridden in one. And Buddy rode very well for us at Washington and here. He's still just a shade over being a junior. He's only 18 and his trip with us this summer was his first exposure to international competition. Their performances portend well for the future of our team."[19]

CHAPTER 14

CLEVELAND BOUND

After contributing to two consecutive Nations Cup victories, Sandsablaze enjoyed some well-earned time off during the winter months. As he had in previous years, Pappy spent the winter, as Brown says, "just being a horse," turned out in a four-acre field with the Browns' other show horses. His shoes were pulled, and he enjoyed frolicking in the snowy fields, decked out in a New Zealand Rug for warmth, with A Little Bit and other herdmates. As the spring approached, the Browns brought Pappy back slowly, with Graham often riding him on the flat and building the horse's muscles by walking him up and down hills.

As Brown was riding several other horses—and as Pappy had proven himself as a consistent competitor—he opted to wait until summer to begin actively campaigning Sandsablaze. In July, the pair traveled to Canada for the "Man and His World" horse show in scenic Montreal. At that competition, Sandsablaze put on a bit of a show for the crowds. A morning rainfall had resulted in a muddy course, which caused Pappy to struggle in the deep and uneven footing. Nevertheless, he jumped clean and was one of only three horses to qualify for the jump-off. After clearing the first element of a dicey triple combination in the jump-off, however, the little horse fell down on all fours, unseating Brown in the process. As the crowd watched in amazement, Sandsablaze rose to his feet and—apparently unaware that Brown was no longer on his back—continued to jump the remaining two elements of the triple combination sans rider. Since the pair had jumped clear in the prior rounds, Brown and Sandsablaze captured the bronze medal behind

Canada's hometown hero, Frank Selinger, and Anthony d'Ambrosio of the United States.

Later that summer, Brown and Sandsablaze traveled to Ohio to compete in the Chagrin Valley PHA Horse Show in July. The competition was held at the Metropolitan Polo Field in Moreland Hills, a suburb of Cleveland. The Cleveland Grand Prix, held annually at this horse show, was one of the oldest outdoor grand prix competitions in the nation and, in fact, was the first U.S. grand prix open to international, amateur and professional riders. The course was designed by Jerry Baker of Cleveland, with assistance from Robert Jolicoeur, who developed a highly difficult test of sixteen obstacles measuring nearly six feet apiece. These included a liverpool that extended ten feet wide, an extended open-water jump, a "huge and threatening" peak called the Osborne Bank and the main attraction of the course—the famed Cleveland wall. Coach Bert de Némethy, in observing the jumps, noted that the fences were "bigger than we will see in the Olympics."

In addition to Brown, whose mounts at Cleveland also included A Little Bit and Aries, several other USET riders were entered in the jumper divisions. These included Rodney Jenkins on Idle Dice and Number One Spy, Melanie Smith on Crimson Tide and Radnor II, Conrad Homfeld on Mystic and Balbuco and Michael Matz on Grande and Mighty Ruler. Joey Darby, who had trained Sandsablaze as a young horse for Pappy and Ginnie Moss, would compete in the grand prix aboard Arrive Alive.

On July 24, at the onset of the jumper events, Brown and Sandsablaze competed in an open jumper class in front of a crowd of seven thousand spectators. For the first time in the horse show's history, there was a tie for the open jumper championship, as Sandsablaze and Idle Dice completed the course in a virtual dead heat. Brown rode first, clearing all of the obstacles in a scorching 38.1 seconds, followed by Jenkins, who duplicated the clear performance in the same exact time. Following in third was Melanie Smith aboard Radnor II, who finished the course in 38.9 seconds, with Conrad Homfeld and the legendary Balbuco clocking in at 39.5 seconds.

The highlight of the horse show, the Cleveland Grand Prix, was held on the following Sunday, with Brown and Sandsablaze slated as the twenty-sixth of forty entries. A local Cleveland newspaper, in an attempt to add some amusement to the event, decided to handicap the field by assigning odds to each horse-rider pair. Brown and Sandsablaze were listed at betting odds of 5–1, well behind the designated favorites, Idle Dice (1–1) and Number One Spy (2–1), both ridden by Rodney Jenkins. Other odds-on favorites included Caesar and Joe Fargis, fresh off a victory in the Adirondack

Grand Prix, and Michele McEvoy and Sundancer, two-time winners of the American Invitational. After publishing these odds in the daily newspaper, the Cleveland media noted that the article was all in fun. "Handicapping grand prix," the *Cleveland Plain Dealer* quipped, "is mostly a guessing game."[20]

The footing in the grand prix ring at Cleveland was to Sandsablaze's liking—firm and without give—and Brown was able to gain a feel for the course when he rode A Little Bit in the earlier part of the round. Brown and Sandsablaze tackled the winding course with polish and flair, posting a clean trip in the opening round. As one of a number of horse-rider combinations without any faults, the pair would take to the grueling course a total of three times. To the surprise and dismay of the crowd, the legendary Idle Dice pulled a rail in the second round, knocking him well out of contention for the win and paving the way for a possible upset.

After three rounds over the daunting course, only two combinations had posted triple clear rounds: Joe Fargis aboard Caesar and Buddy Brown on Sandsablaze. Fargis was first of the two to take to the final round, posting a clear round over Baker's course in 56.2 seconds. It was then time for Buddy and Sandsablaze, who, according to the media, "came whipping around the course" in 53.3 seconds, well ahead of the time previously posted by Fargis. As Brown and Pappy cleared the final fence on course—the formidable Cleveland

Buddy and Sandsablaze jump the famed Cleveland Wall en route to winning the 1975 Cleveland Grand Prix. *Photo courtesy of Chagrin Valley PHA Horse Shows Inc.*

Sandsablaze's half brother, San Man, shown here with Meredith McLaughlin, was a top show hunter and equitation horse. *Photo courtesy of Meredith McLaughlin.*

Wall—the crowd rose to its feet, cheering wildly for the teenager and his trusty bright chestnut mount. "Buddy Brown and Sandsablaze upset all the big boys Sunday," heralded the *Cleveland Plain Dealer*, noting that the pair "bested the highly favored Joe Fargis and Caesar in a blistering round of fences." The newspaper continued in its praise for Brown and his mount. "Those attending Sunday's finale, the Cleveland Grand Prix," it wrote, "had a fine day with the extra thrill of an upset victory by young Buddy Brown aboard a horse with the gorgeous name of Sandsablaze."[21]

Interestingly, while Sandsablaze was galloping to victory in the grand prix ring, another chestnut gelding was dominating the hunter classes at the very same event. That horse was none other than Sandsablaze's half brother, San Man, who dominated in the hunter ring with junior rider Colette Lozins. The *Cleveland Plain Dealer*, unaware of the relation, noted, "San Man, another U.S. champion, continued his winning ways, gaining the championship for small junior hunters. Thus the 15.3 hand chestnut prolongs his unbeaten string of tri-colors."[22] The following season, San Man would win the ASPCA Maclay finals with Lozins in the saddle, three years after Buddy and Sandsablaze had won the AHSA Medal. The two half brothers would forever be linked as champions in the highest levels of the sport.

CHAPTER 15

PAN AM GLORY

Following their victory in the Cleveland Grand Prix, Brown and Sandsablaze were selected to represent the United States at the Pan American (Pan Am) Games. Established in 1951 in Buenos Aires, the Pan Am Games are an Olympic-type competition open to athletes from forty-two nations within South, Central and North America, as well as the Caribbean. Similar to the Olympics, the Pan Am Games offer athletes the opportunity to win gold, silver and bronze medals in various sports, including the equestrian disciplines of show jumping, eventing and dressage. The games are held once every four years in the year preceding the summer Olympics.

The 1975 Pan Am Games were held in Mexico City, which became the first place to hold the games on more than one occasion, having hosted the event previously in 1955. The 1975 games were originally assigned to Chile; however, after the assassination of President Salvador Allende in 1973, political turmoil and economic problems led Chile to withdraw as host city, leaving Mexico City to step up in a short timeframe to host the games. From October 12 through 26, approximately 3,146 athletes from thirty-three countries gathered in Mexico City to compete in nineteen different sports.

In order to get the horses acclimated to the altitude change, the team traveled to Mexico City five weeks in advance of the games. Mexico City is located eight thousand feet above sea level, and in the past, the USET had found that such changes in altitude could impact horses' heart and respiration rates while working. As such, veterinarians advised that horses be acclimated to the high altitudes before embarking on any competitive event.

Due to the climate in Mexico City, the daytime hours were exceptionally hot. As a result, the horses were worked in the early morning hours when the temperatures were more bearable.

Sandsablaze and the other horses traveled well, arriving at Mexico City with time to spare. Brown was selected to compete in both the individual and team finals, along with teammates Michael Matz, Dennis Murphy and Joe Fargis. Brown brought A Little Bit along for the individual events and would ride the more consistent Sandsablaze in the team competition. The grey gelding A Little Bit performed exceptionally well, clinching the individual silver medal for Brown, while Matz earned the individual bronze aboard Grande. Mexican Fernando Senderos won the gold aboard the great Jet Run, who would subsequently be sold to U.S. businessman F. Eugene Dixon and earn fame with Michael Matz in the saddle.

The team jumping events took place in the Aztec Stadium on the final day of competition and were, in fact, the last events held prior to the closing ceremonies. On the previous night, Mexico had lost a soccer game, and a riot had ensued, ushering in a shower of anti-American sentiment. The crowd of 125,000 erupted in hostility as the USET battled the Mexican team for the gold medal. While Brown and Sandsablaze had been virtual unknowns on the international show jumping scene just one year before, they had since proven themselves as formidable threats to snatch the gold medal away from the favored Mexican team.

In the first two rounds of competition, the course had challenged the best horses and riders, with only a handful of clear rounds posted from a deep well of talent. One obstacle—a wide water jump late on course—posed particular problems for many of the teams. In the final round, which would determine the medals, Brown and Sandsablaze served in their familiar role as the team anchors and were the last to represent the U.S. on course. Their performance in that round would determine the gold medalists for the team event. The Mexican team, led by Senderos on Jet Run, had performed quite well, leaving the United States with little room for mistakes. Brown and Sandsablaze could post no more than four faults in order to secure the gold for their team.

Graham Brown recalls hearing thundering boos from the crowd as Buddy and Sandsablaze entered the arena. Angry Mexicans flashed the lights on and off in a display of hostility toward the U.S. team. Sandsablaze held his composure, despite the antagonism around him, and remained his usual, calm self. The activity of the crowd energized rather than intimidated the horse as he and Brown began their signature changes of lead. Brown saluted the judges and tipped his hat to the crowd, which caused the angry Mexicans to erupt with jeers. Brown recalls that the booing and stomping from the masses was so strong that "it sounded as if the stadium were about to come tumbling down."

The air was thick with pressure as Brown and Sandsablaze made their way around the course. As the horse cleared each fence, Brown's thoughts turned to the final three obstacles: a straight finish beginning with a large vertical, with approximately eight strides to the aforementioned water jump and the final fence, an oxer, on the other side near the finish. Brown was concerned that Sandsablaze might underestimate the width of the water and under-jump it, which would result in him not being properly set up to clear the last fence. Brown was not about to spoil the USET's gold medal chances by accumulating eight faults on the last two jumps and thus made a bold and risky decision. Realizing that Sandsablaze would likely gain four faults on the water jump, Brown would allow the horse to canter through the water in order to have a better approach to the final fence. "I somehow thought that I could not risk having that last jump down," Brown later said, "and I was not sure we could get over the water. So I decided to go with another plan."

Brown's teammates watched from the sidelines, holding their collective breath as Sandsablaze cantered through the water. Unaware of Brown's plan, the anti-American crowd erupted with joy as four faults appeared on the score screen, hoping that the little horse would proceed to knock down the final fence. Brown, however, had other plans. Riding tactfully according to plan, he and Sandsablaze boldly cleared the last obstacle, securing the gold medal for the U.S. team. As they left the arena, a jubilant Brown petted his horse, tipped his hat and then pumped his fist in exhilaration when he saw his U.S. teammates on the sidelines. The irate Mexican spectators did not appreciate that gesture in the least; the crowd collectively rose to its feet, chanting "Mexico" and stomping the ground with anger and contempt. For the safety of horses and riders, event officials told the U.S. team to pack up and leave the stadium; they would receive their gold medals at a later date.

Once again, Brown and Sandsablaze were elevated to hero status as they secured yet another victory for the USET. Amid all the pressure and hostility around him, Brown reached a rite of passage. As he and Sandsablaze galloped around that course, Brown's self-esteem had increased substantially. At that moment, on the world's stage, the once-shy teenager had become a man.

Right: Buddy poses with one of his medals won at the 1975 Pan Am Games. *Photo courtesy of the USET Foundation*.

Below: Buddy had a strategic plan for Sandsablaze and the water jump at the 1975 Pan Am Games. *Photo courtesy of the USET Foundation*.

After returning home, Brown and Sandsablaze represented the United States at yet another Nations Cup event at the 1975 National Horse Show. According to the media, the event was "practically settled" in the afternoon round, when Buddy piloted Sandsablaze to a perfect trip around the course after clear rounds by Michael Matz on Grande, Dennis Murphy on Do Right and Rodney Jenkins on Idle Dice. Heading into the evening round, the United States had completed a whopping sixty-four fences without garnering a single fault. Only one other rider—Daniel Constant of France aboard Vicomte Aubiner—had posted a clear round over the course.

Coach Bert de Némethy stated, "We had a meeting for about five minutes before the first round. I didn't give the riders any special instructions. They all know their assignments. After all, with the exception of Rod Jenkins, it was our Pan-American team, and with the way Jenkins had been going, we were confident. This is the most important class of the show to us. It's the one that will show on the scoreboard when the other international teams in Europe start measuring us up."

In the evening, Buddy and Sandsablaze once again anchored the U.S. team due to their obvious ability to remain calm under pressure. Brown recalls that Sandsablaze was de Némethy's example of a "perfect Nations Cup horse," since he never refused fences and typically accumulated four faults or fewer per round. More often than not, Sandsablaze jumped clean in Nations Cup rounds. This round at Madison Square Garden was no exception, as Brown and Sandsablaze completed the course without a single flaw, following a similarly perfect round by Michael Matz aboard Grande. While Dennis Murphy garnered four faults when Do Right knocked down a red-and-white rail, the team had amassed these mere four faults in a total of 109 jumping efforts. That evening, the USET captured yet another Nations Cup, well ahead of competitors Canada, France and Poland. The *New York Times* summed up the victory best, noting, "The performance of the USET was simply outstanding."

CHAPTER 16
JUMPING TO NEW HEIGHTS

Following their latest victory at New York, Buddy and Sandsablaze traveled with the USET to the Royal Winter Fair in Toronto, Canada, where they would compete for another Nations Cup. Joining the pair in Toronto were teammates Ridland, Murphy and Jenkins. The competition began on a high note, as both Brown on Sandsablaze and Murphy aboard Do Right posted clear rounds in the afternoon. In the evening, Sandsablaze repeated his flawless performance, leading the USET to yet another team victory.

Following this win, Sandsablaze demonstrated his versatility in several different types of events. In a speed class on November 19, Pappy confirmed that he could gallop with the best and was only narrowly beaten at the clock by Belgium's Eric Wauters aboard Pomme d'Api. Robert Ridland and Rodney Jenkins, aboard Southside and Idle Dice, respectively, finished sixth and seventh in this class.

Sandsablaze further proved his adaptability as he competed in the International Relay event. In this class, each rider completes a course of eight fences on two different mounts (in this case, Buddy competed on Sandsablaze and A Little Bit). Both horses are brought into the ring together, with the rider astride one animal and a groom leading the other horse. After the rider completes the course with his first mount, he quickly switches over to the second and completes the course in a reverse pattern. The event was ultimately won by Moffat Dunlap of Canada, who captured the first victory of the show for Canada with his mounts, Cousin Albert and Scotch Valley. Brown finished a respectable fourth, which was the top placing of the U.S. entries.

While the team's performance placed it in the running for the overall championship at Toronto, Coach de Némethy was concerned that there were other countries in close contention. De Némethy soon developed an idea to gain additional points for the U.S. team. Robert Ridland and Almost Persuaded, who had won the puissance at Wembley in 1974, were chosen to enter the popular class, an event similar to an equestrian high jumping competition. The name "puissance" is fittingly derived from the French word meaning "power." The event, which is not timed, involves jumping two obstacles: a spread fence and a huge, intimidating brick wall that becomes progressively higher after each successful jumping effort. The starting height for the wall is typically five feet, eleven inches, with bricks added to raise the wall by several inches after each round. The event may reach a maximum of four jump-offs over the wall, with a tie finish called at the end of four rounds if more than one horse and rider has cleared the fence.

In addition to Ridland and his mount, de Némethy chose Brown and Sandsablaze to represent the United States in the puissance event. Brown was admittedly concerned, as Pappy had no experience in jumping tall, solid, single fences and would likely be eliminated after one or two efforts. De Némethy instructed Brown not to worry, as the team would accumulate the sought-after points even if they cleared only the first two attempts. If the wall were to become dangerously high, the pair could simply withdraw from the event.

Also entered in the puissance that day were Eric Wauters and his horse Pomme d'Api, who held the existing world outdoor puissance record of seven feet, six inches. Brown and Ridland, both riding smallish Thoroughbreds, were a bit intimidated to compete against this experienced duo. Prior to the start of the class, the two U.S. riders made a side bet—the first to knock down the puissance wall would owe the other five dollars.

As he had in the past, Sandsablaze stepped up for the occasion, clearing the intimidating brick wall with determination as it rose to six feet, six inches. Ridland on Almost Persuaded also went clear, with both riders earning points for the U.S. team. After several attempts, Coach de Némethy decided that they had accumulated enough points and would withdraw from the class rather than taxing the horses any further. To his surprise, however, a new rule had been enacted whereby horses and riders would be unable to withdraw unless either had sustained an injury. The reasoning behind the

Buddy and Sandsablaze clear the massive puissance wall at the Royal Winter Fair in Toronto in 1975. *Photo by R.J. Maynard of Vancouver, Canada; courtesy of Joey Darby.*

new rule was such that the puissance was designed to entertain the crowds, and there would be much disappointment on the part of the spectators if teams were simply allowed to bow out. Under the rules of the competition, the wall would be elevated two more times. When it was raised the first time, to six feet, ten inches, Brown and Sandsblaze went clean once more, as did Ridland and Wauters on their respective mounts. The wall was then raised to its final height of seven feet, one inch.

The monstrous wall looked Brown in the eye as he galloped Pappy around the arena. The teenager attempted to maintain his focus as he jumped the warm-up fence and then cantered across the diagonal and toward the enormous brick-filled wall. With trepidation, Brown guided Sandsablaze toward the obstacle, which now towered over them. As they headed toward the jump, Brown felt a change in the horse's demeanor. "Normally, Pappy was incredibly lazy," he said. "But when he saw that wall, he grabbed the bit and galloped towards it. There was probably not even enough space to fit a piece of paper between him and the top of the wall, but he cleared it."

The crowd sprang to its feet, amazed at the heart of the game little Thoroughbred. After all three horses cleared the wall at seven feet, one inch, the show officials called an end to the event, with Brown, Ridland and Wauters sharing first-place honors. "I was scared to death," Brown later told the media. "I just took the fences like I was in dreamland. I'd say, 'There comes another' and not think."

For his part, Sandsablaze seemed proud of his efforts, standing confidently as yet another blue ribbon was affixed to his bridle. The little horse that was deemed unable to jump above three feet, six inches had added another chapter to his fairytale story.

CHAPTER 17

OLYMPIC SPIRIT

For any athlete in any sport, the Olympic Games represent the pinnacle of pride and achievement. There is something unique about the Olympic events, which unite athletes from all over the world in a celebration of sport and spirit. It was no surprise, then, that Brown was elated when he was chosen to represent the United States in the 1976 Olympics in Montreal, Canada. Also included on the team were Brown's friends Robert Ridland, Michael Matz and Dennis Murphy, with Frank Chapot serving once again as the team captain.

In preparation for the Olympics, Brown and Sandsablaze had returned with the U.S. team to Europe in order to gain some momentum heading into the games and to face off against the best horses and riders in the world. Sandsablaze, having already proven himself among the most consistent of the USET mounts, competed in the Nations Cup events, while Brown rode his other horses in the individual grand prix events. By this time, Brown had gained the ride on the talented French horse Viscount, who had been purchased for the USET by Jane and Raymond Firestone. Brown had competed successfully on the French gelding on the Florida circuit and, in Europe, placed third in the prestigious Grand Prix of Aachen. On that same tour, Brown and A Little Bit won the Grand Prix of Wiesbaden. As Brown now had three grand prix mounts (Sandsablaze, A Little Bit and Viscount) to his name and would require only two for the Olympic Games, he opted to give up the ride on Viscount. In the Olympics, Viscount would be ridden by the legendary Frank Chapot.

The Olympic show jumping events included two separate classes: one for individuals and another for team jumping. As he had in the Pan Am Games the previous year, Brown chose to ride A Little Bit in the individual event, while the more consistent Sandsablaze would compete in the team events. The individual events were held at the newly constructed equestrian stadium in Bromont, while the team jumping would take place in the main Olympic stadium, the site of the opening and closing ceremonies.

Despite some political turmoil at this time, a total of twenty-three nations competed at the 1976 Olympics. Chile and Poland were not allowed to ship their horses to Canada due to health concerns, while veterinary regulations also prevented the shipment of some horses from Italy and France. For the first time in history, a horse was disqualified from the games due to a positive drug test, as San Carlos, the entry of Ireland's Ronald McMahon, had received a forbidden treatment during transport. The United States had no such issues or restrictions, and Sandsablaze and the other U.S. horses enjoyed an uneventful journey north to Montreal.

The course was designed by Tom Gayford, with assistance from the famed Robert Jolicoeur, and consisted of fifteen jumping obstacles, including a water jump measuring five meters in width. The course presented a twisting round of boldness and skill, designed to test the world's best horses and riders over narrow verticals, huge oxers and formidable brush jumps. The team jumping included two rounds of competition, with the fences raised in height after the first round.

In preparation for the event on August 1, a fresh layer of sod had been placed on the stadium course, which, when coupled with intense, rainy conditions, resulted in a deep, wet "carpet" of mud. There was discussion involving the shifting of the team events to Bromont, where conditions would be better; however, officials in the end decided to hold the events at the stadium as planned. Robert Ridland remembers that it felt like "riding on wet carpet," noting that the footing caused difficulty for all of the horses. Due to the immense height of the jumps and the footing on that day, not a single clear round was posted in the Nations Cup competition.

The soggy, deep footing was tough for Sandsablaze to maneuver, and he and Brown completed the first round with an uncharacteristic twelve faults. Frank Chapot aboard Viscount also posted twelve faults, while Michael Matz and Robert Ridland each accumulated sixteen faults, placing the team in seventh place overall. Ridland recalls that the team rallied for a chance at a medal. "We scraped and clawed our way into the second round. We were seventh after the first round, with only the

Sandsablaze tried his best in the 1976 Olympics despite less-than-favorable conditions. *Photo by Karl Leck.*

top eight moving on to round two," he said. As the footing deteriorated throughout the course of the event, Sandsablaze struggled a bit, posting sixteen faults in the second round, while Ridland and Chapot knocked only one rail apiece. Matz's horse, Grande, also struggled with the footing, adding twenty-four faults to the total. However, as only the top three scores would count, the team finished with a total of twenty-four faults. As so many horses and riders were struggling, this was actually the third-best team score of the round. The best overall performance was posted by West Germany's Alwin Schockemöhle, who completed the two rounds with four and eight faults, respectively.

Nevertheless, the U.S. team that Ridland described as "scrappy" had boosted itself to a game fourth-place finish, narrowly missing out on a medal behind France, West Germany and Belgium. Brown was proud of Sandsablaze's valiant effort, as the horse had tried his hardest despite the less-than-favorable conditions. Brown worried that Sandsablaze might have injured himself, as he had shown some difficulty swapping leads in the deep mud. He did not show any unsoundness, however, as the team prepared for the trip home.

A couple days later, after returning to the States, Brown received a call from Coach de Némethy. The coach was concerned that Sandsablaze's tendon was warm and swollen, and the veterinarian would soon be on hand to examine him. The vet's results determined that Pappy had indeed bowed a tendon and would require almost a year off to heal.

Buddy and Sandsablaze finished fourth as part of the U.S. team in the 1976 Olympic Games. *Photo courtesy of Karl Leck.*

Left: Buddy and Sandsablaze land after a jump at the 1976 Olympic Games. *Photo by Karl Leck*.

Below: Teammate Robert Ridland noted that Sandsablaze was the "epitome of the Olympic spirit" of the USET in 1976. *Photo by Karl Leck*.

While the USET had not brought home an Olympic medal from Montreal, the team had proven that it could compete with the best in the world. Sandsablaze, in particular, had proved that he possessed the heart of a champion, competing bravely despite suffering what was later revealed to be a serious injury. Teammate Robert Ridland best summed up Pappy's great heart. "Sandsablaze never gave up at the Olympics. No matter what, he kept on trying," he said. "Sandsablaze truly embodied the spirit of our entire Olympic team at that time."

CHAPTER 18
BETTER THAN EVER

S andsablaze recovered from his injury in due time, with Brown bringing him back slowly to ensure that the horse was fully healed. He returned to competition in the summer of 1977 at the Lake Placid Horse Show, where he competed in an open hunter classic to avoid undue stress on his tendon. Brown did not want to push Sandsablaze too hard by entering him in the jumper ring, opting instead for a working hunter course to avoid tight turns and speed. The pair competed in the hunter classic over fences measuring up to four feet, six inches in height, earning a fourth-place ribbon among some of the nation's leading show hunters. Again, Pappy demonstrated his incredible versatility, as a typical grand prix jumper would not usually remain quiet enough to return successfully to the hunter ring.

As Sandsablaze had not competed in the grand prix ring in over a year, he was eligible to begin his return to the jumper division at a lower, less strenuous level. At the Chagrin PHA Horse Show in Cleveland that summer, Brown competed Pappy as an intermediate jumper, claiming championship honors for the division. As he became stronger and his fitness level improved, Sandsablaze was back in the grand prix ring for the indoor circuit, with Brown expecting to compete him only lightly. By this time, Brown had gained back the ride on Viscount and had planned to compete him at the indoor shows that year; however, that plan was foiled when the horse developed a lameness issue. In an effort to boost the U.S. team, Sandsablaze made his return to the USET in early October at the Washington International Horse Show.

Buddy and Sandsablaze returned to the show ring in the summer of 1977 in a hunter classic at the Lake Placid Horse Show. This is Buddy's favorite photograph of Pappy. *Photo by JJ Walsh, courtesy of Buddy Brown.*

To the eyes of the spectators at the Capital Center, it was difficult to imagine that Sandsablaze had just returned from an injury; the horse was performing better than ever. In the opening international open jumper class, Buddy and Sandsablaze bested teammates Dennis Murphy and Tuscaloosa by a mere one-tenth of a second to claim the blue ribbon and trophy for the class. The pair led a U.S. sweep in this class, with Murphy second, Rodney Jenkins placing third aboard Wasted Words and Michael Matz on Grande rounding out the fourth spot. Tim Grubb of the UK and Terri Leibel of Canada rounded out the top six places.

Five days later, on Halloween evening, Brown and Pappy were entered in the President's Cup, the most prestigious event of the WIHS competition. One of the first to tackle the course was Jenkins, aboard the great Idle Dice, the only pair to win the President's Cup in two consecutive years. (Jenkins had also won the event on another occasion, with Number One Spy.) Unfortunately for Jenkins, the great horse snagged a rail in the jump-off to accumulate four faults. Jenkins told the media, "He made a good try, but he just missed one fence. In a class like this, it can kill you."[23]

The next four combinations also accumulated four faults each. These included three other U.S. entries—Dennis Murphy and Do Right, Robert Ridland and Southside and Bernie Traurig and the Cardinal—along with West Germany's Willibert Mehlkopf aboard Fantast. Michael Matz accumulated three faults aboard Jet Run, due to the strapping Thoroughbred's refusal at one fence. It was now up to Brown and Sandsablaze, and the pair focused on the task at hand. They cleared fence after fence without fault, posting the only clear round of the jump-off. The President's Cup was now added to the pair's growing list of victories. Brown later told the media, "I always figure Sandsablaze has a good shot. He's jumped well in Washington in the past, has been going very good all year and was in good form tonight."[24]

By the show's end, the U.S. riders had proven their dominance, winning eight of the international jumper classes and accumulating 110 points for the team. As such, the U.S. team—which included Brown, Matz, Conrad

Buddy and Sandsablaze pose with their blue ribbon after winning the President's Cup at the Washington International Horse Show in 1977. *Photo courtesy of Joey Darby.*

Homfeld and Joe Fargis—captured the Nations Cup for the fifth straight year at WIHS.

Days later, at Madison Square Garden, Sandsablaze continued his winning streak at the National Horse Show. With back-to-back clean rounds, he and Brown captured the Whitney Stone Trophy, named for the past president of the American Horse Shows Association. In the first round, Pappy competed against seventeen other horses, with six horses in total jumping clean around the course. Prior to Sandsablaze's entrance in the arena, teammate Michael Matz had posted a fantastic round, clearing the course in 38.0 seconds flat with no faults aboard the legendary Jet Run. Terri Leibel of Canada had also gone clean but was unable to best Matz's time, clocking in at 38.6 seconds aboard Merchant of Venice.

Brown remembers, "I didn't know what Michael's time was, but I knew he had cut his corners sharp. I was determined to go as clean as I could. And every time I made a turn, the opportunity was there for the next turn."[25] Buddy and Sandsablaze cleared the course of nine obstacles in 36.5 seconds, marking the pair's fourth consecutive win, having won three at WIHS the week before, and their sixth in their last twelve events. The *New York Times* proudly proclaimed in the next day's newspaper, "Sandsablaze Extends Winning Streak as Jumper."

Following this latest victory, Buddy and Pappy contributed to another Nations Cup win for the United States, jumping clear in three consecutive rounds of competition. When jump-offs were added to the total, Brown recalls, Sandsablaze had jumped eighteen consecutive clear rounds. When asked about the pair's strategy, Brown explained, "We still give him days off as much as we can. But once he gets in gear, he's sound all the way." The young man later noted, "Sandsablaze is my favorite horse. He is a complete horse. This year he has won three grand prix events and just about everything else too. I have been riding him for seven years. Now he will get a nice rest."[26]

As evidence of his popularity at this time, Sandsablaze was included in two published books. In addition to several photographs in George Morris's classic *Hunter Seat Equitation*, Sandsablaze was featured in William Steinkraus's book, *Great Horses of the U.S. Equestrian Team*. The book, published in 1977 by Dodd, Mead & Company, included two drawings of Sandsablaze by the legendary equine artist Sam Savitt.

As Brown was now riding several other top horses (including Viscount) in grand prix events, he opted to compete Sandsablaze on a less frequent basis. The 1978 and 1979 seasons were rather uneventful, although Sandsablaze was consistently in the ribbons in most of his classes. When Viscount

Buddy and Sandsablaze were crowd favorites during their years on the grand prix circuit. *Photo courtesy of the USET Foundation.*

sustained a career-ending injury in 1978, Sandsablaze once again stepped up for the team. Among his other accomplishments, Sandsablaze helped the USET secure the win in the Nations Cup at the National Horse Show in New York. The following spring, he and Brown were chosen to compete at their second Pan American Games. This time, the competition was held in San Juan, Puerto Rico, in early July. The games lasted fifteen days and were attended by 3,700 competitors from thirty-four countries.

Joining Brown and Sandsablaze on the team were Norman Dello Joio on Allegro, Melanie Smith aboard Val de Loire and Michael Matz riding Jet Run. The team jumping event was the first of the equestrian events, and the USET excelled over two grueling rounds. Sandsablaze, now twelve years old, rose to the challenge, helping lead the USET to yet another team gold medal. The team finished with only 34.5 penalty points for the competition, as compared to Canada's 66.0 points for the silver medal and Mexico's 100.2 points for the bronze. Brown and Sandsablaze, as a team, had now earned gold medals at two different Pan Am Games.

CHAPTER 19
TRIUMPH AND TRAGEDY

Fresh off of their gold medal–winning performance in the Pan Am Games, Buddy and Sandsablaze headed to Branchville, New Jersey, to compete in the Garden State Grand Prix on August 12. The event had attracted many of the nation's leading riders, including Brown's Pan Am teammates Michael Matz, Melanie Smith and Norman Dello Joio. The course at Garden State was challenging; after the first round of competition, only Brown and Dello Joio had posted clear rounds. The two former teammates would head into a jump-off to determine who would emerge as the victor.

Dello Joio rode the course first on the ten-year-old bay gelding Allegro, catching one rail for a total of four faults. If Brown and Sandsablaze could post a clear round, they would win yet another grand prix class. Brown skillfully guided the flashy gelding around the twisting, turning course as he had done so many times in their eight-year partnership. The pair cleared each fence in harmony, demonstrating the skill and partnership that had characterized their incredible success. The crowd was hushed in excitement as the pair cleared the final fence without a single fault, the rhythmic clap of Sandsablaze's gallant hooves the only sound to be heard.

Suddenly, as he and Sandsablaze landed and galloped toward the finish line, Brown heard an odd and frightening noise. It was, as he recalls, similar to the sound of a baseball bat cracking in half as it is broken against a tree. In an instant, young Brown concluded exactly what that sound meant: Sandsablaze had more than likely injured his leg. Summoning every bit of his strength, Brown pulled on the reins and braced his body in the saddle to stop the heroic horse; Sandsablaze, driven by adrenaline and the excitement of the crowd, galloped bravely through the flags and past the finish line.

In a blur, Brown jumped off to the side, and the impulsion sent him landing against a wishing well–shaped jump standard. Onlookers raced into the ring to see what they could do. One of the first was Brown's friend Robin Rost Fairclough, who was watching the class from the sidelines when the accident occurred. Fairclough happened to be standing near the final jump when she heard the startling sound of the break. In an instant, Fairclough hopped the fence into the arena, where she grabbed Sandsablaze's reins and helped Brown to his feet.

Dr. John Lowe, the veterinarian assigned to the horse show, and the USET veterinarian, Dr. Allen Leslie, quickly made their way into the ring to examine the ailing champion. Both Brown and Fairclough remember that, before the doctors spoke a single word, they could tell that the injury was severe. It was a high fracture of the left foreleg, at the top part of the cannon bone, and was visible to the naked eye despite the fact that the horse was wearing rundowns. Fairclough held the gelding's reins, soothing him as Brown attempted to gain his composure. Buddy remembers that Sandsablaze "stood there with his leg in the air. He wore rundowns because of his tendon injury, but you could see under them that he had broken his leg."[27]

The veterinarian administered an anesthetic to lessen the pain as he examined Sandsablaze's injured leg. While there was initial talk of loading the horse into a trailer, it was determined that the injury was too severe to transport Sandsablaze to a veterinary hospital. There was no other choice but to end the animal's suffering. First, the winner's trophy would be presented before the crowds; the stands would subsequently be emptied of spectators before the final injection was administered. Both Brown and Fairclough remember that day as if it were yesterday. "He was calm and fine and just standing there," Brown remembers. "So we did the awards ceremony around him. He stood there with his ears up. The crowd left, and we put him down right there in the ring."[28]

If one had not looked upon his damaged leg, it would appear that the champion horse was simply standing at attention. Sandsablaze let out a deep-sounded whinney and stood, ears pricked, with his head held high. Like the hero that he was, he stood proudly as the winner's trophy was presented for his efforts, retaining his dignity even in these final moments. As the veterinarian prepared the solution that would put the gallant horse to sleep, the crowd was asked to leave and a curtain was placed in front of the animal. The crowd was ushered out of the arena, and Brown was allowed to bid farewell to his cherished equine partner and friend.

The Rost family offered to bury Sandsablaze on their nearby farm, and his final resting place would be alongside Robin's beloved champion jumper, Wiggs Bar. Before the horse's body was loaded into the trailer for transport, the veterinarian removed Sandsablaze's shoes and handed them to Brown.

As anyone who has experienced a sudden loss can understand, Brown was in a daze, trying in earnest to make sense of the events that had just befallen him. He had lost not only his partner in the sport but also a dear friend. In respect for that partnership, Brown accepted the trophy on behalf of his beloved horse. It was a testament to the character of the young man, who, traveling without his family, had to make a heartbreaking phone call to his parents. When his father answered the telephone at home, Brown, choking back tears, had to deliver the most painful news that had befallen his young life. Pappy had won the grand prix, and now he was gone.

Shortly after Sandsablaze's untimely passing, Graham Brown wrote a poignant tribute that was published in the *Chronicle of the Horse*. It read as follows:

SANDSABLAZE
1967–1979

By Graham G. Brown

On Sunday, August 12, a Cinderella horse in international show jumping was lost—Sandsablaze landed poorly over the final fence in the jump-off of the Garden State Grand Prix at the Sussex County (NJ) Horse Show. He finished on three legs to gain a final victory, but Sandsablaze was humanely put down shortly thereafter when it was determined that a cannon bone had been fractured.

Sandsablaze was foaled in Illinois in 1967, bred by William L. Manis, and he was a chestnut with four high white stockings, a big blaze and a splash of white on his belly. He was sired by Blazing Count, who was a son of the immortal Count Fleet, and Blazing Count was second to Nashua in the 1955 running of the Belmont Stakes. Sandsablaze was produced by Sandy Atlas, a daughter of Ladysman, and Sandy Atlas enjoyed an enviable racing career—in eight seasons, she went to the post no fewer than 125 times, winning 18 races and finishing either second or third on 37 occasions.

As a two-year-old, Sandsablaze (which was his registered name) was consigned to a bloodstock sale in Kentucky, where he was purchased by the late W.O. (Pappy) Moss, the MFH of the Moore County Hounds in North Carolina. At three, Mr. Moss placed Sandsablaze in the hands of Joey Darby, and Sandsablaze was subsequently sold to Sally Walker of Tryon (NC), who played with her purchase for the balance of his three-year-old year.

The Brown family (of Pound Ridge, NY) bought the 16-hand Sandsablaze in 1971 as a junior hunter for 15-year-old Buddy Brown. It soon became apparent, however, that Sandsablaze was not destined to make history in show hunter ranks—he simply didn't provide a sufficiently attractive hunter picture over fences, and Buddy and Sandsablaze made their debut the following year in the jumper division, competing in the junior and preliminary divisions, and he immediately displayed heart and enthusiasm for big fences. We nicknamed him "Pappy," in honor of Mr. Moss, and "Pappy" and Buddy won their first class in the preliminary division that summer at Lake Placid.

In the fall of 1973, "Pappy" momentarily deserted the jumper division, being used as Buddy's mount in winning the AHSA Hunter Seat Medal finals at Harrisburg. The following year, "Pappy" was the horse that secured Buddy's selection to ride with the USET's Prix de Nation squad. At the time, Buddy was 18, the youngest rider in history to be chosen. On their first visit to Europe, they won the Grand Prix of Ireland at the Dublin Horse Show.

In 1975, Sandsablaze won the Cleveland Grand Prix, and it was his performance for the USET in the Pan American Games that clinched the gold medal for the U.S. That fall, "Pappy" won the puissance class at the Royal Winter Fair, jumping 7' 1½". The following year, "Pappy" and Buddy represented the United States at the Olympics in Montreal. Then, in 1977, after recovering from an injury sustained at the Olympics, Sandsablaze reeled in victories in six international classes at the fall indoor circuit, including the President's Cup at Washington. In the past two seasons, Sandsablaze contributed to many other USET victories in Nations Cup classes, the latest just last month when he was a member of the gold medal team at the Pan Am Games in Puerto Rico.

Yes, we grieve the loss of our horse, and "Pappy" will undoubtedly be missed by his numerous fans in international show jumping. No one, however, will miss Sandsablaze as much as Buddy Brown.[29]

Sandsablaze was Buddy Brown's "horse of a lifetime." *Photo by Karl Leck.*

Sandsablaze was not the most talented horse in equestrian sports, nor was he the fastest or the most agile. There have been many horses, before and afterward, who exceeded him in all of those regards. Yet the truest sign of a champion is not athletic ability but heart—an attribute that Sandsablaze possessed in spades.

There was also another intangible element that propelled Sandsablaze to grand prix greatness. Former groom Jimmy Herring believes that the secret to Sandsablaze's unparalleled success was his tremendous partnership with and trust in Buddy Brown. This sentiment is echoed by many others in the equestrian world, including those who competed with the pair on Nations Cup and Olympic teams. Sandsablaze's memory thus stands—nearly thirty-five years after his death—as a symbol of the immense strength of the bond between a human and his horse.

For a true horseman such as Buddy Brown, there can be no greater reward.

AFTERWORD

Although this story ends in a tragic way, it was in no way a tragedy to me. Don't get the wrong idea; at the time, it was one of the worst things I had experienced, and I still get choked up when I tell the story. But as I have learned throughout the years, the experiences and memories you have been privileged to share with loved ones that have been lost are all part of the molding of our characters. Pappy was the main character in the making of me as a rider and a horseman.

My journey with Pappy over those years brought us to people and places I could have never imagined possible at such an early time in my life. The four most influential people in my education—Bob Freels, George Morris, Bert de Némethy and my father—were all integral parts of my time with Pappy. We learned together, from hunters to equitation, to jumpers to grand prix, to seven feet, one inch and to the Olympics.

Across that span of time, there were a lot of learning curves we had to overcome, as you have read. To go through all of that with the same horse is unheard of now, and I am not sure if it had happened before. In any case, this was our story. As I look back on those years, the relationship I had with Pappy is more valuable to me than the ribbons and medals. All the "first time" experiences for both of us—traveling all over the world to places we had never been, meeting and competing against legends in the sport and learning that we belonged there—were part of that story.

Pappy's undeniable courage and heart to never stop getting up from a fall or injury showed me a strength at the time that I could count on. Although many steps and lessons we took together were difficult, our trust in each other never wavered. Our youthful ignorance was probably on our side. I have said thousands of times since I have gotten older that I was more frustrated and embarrassed than scared by some of our early falls. Later in my career, I don't know if I would have kept trying as hard as I did back then.

Besides sharing our story together, what I hope this book accomplishes is to help inspire or recommit other riders to their dreams, but mostly to their relationships with their horses. As most of us who have had horses know, they appear strong but are also fragile and can be taken from us without warning in many ways. The other message I have to share is this: despite difficult times and setbacks, if you persevere, you might surprise yourself.

When Pappy and I started our journey together, I could not have imagined where it eventually would take us. He lives with me still to this day—not just in my mind and heart but also on my shoulder. In 2004, I was coming out of semi-retirement from international competition and wanted Pappy with me, so I designed a tattoo with him on it to inspire me. I was not filled with confidence and fearlessness like I was back in the 1970s, and having him back with me really helped. For me, it is a daily reminder, when i see it on my arm each morning, that if you get out there, work hard and stay true to your course, you never know what the day will bring.

I have been blessed with many great horses to ride and work with throughout my career, but I don't think any could have done what Pappy did for me in those years. The lessons we learned from George and Bert still ring in my ears and are a huge part in my riding and teaching to this day.

I was told early on that "horses are for the gods, and it is our luxury to possess them, cherish them, nurture them and, mostly, respect them." Pappy certainly cemented that statement as a truth to me.

Buddy Brown
May 2014

APPENDIX A
OFFSPRING OF SANDY ATLAS

Year	Foal	Gender	Sire	Race Earnings
1957	Sandy Jane	Filly	George Gains	$605
1959	Sandy Barb	Filly	Comte de Grasse	$0
1960	Sissy San	Filly	Comte de Grasse	$16,439
1966	San Man	Colt	Landman	Unraced
1967	Sandsablaze	Colt	Blazing Count	Unraced

PEDIGREE OF SANDSABLAZE

			Sunreigh
		Reigh Count	
			Contessina
	Count Fleet		Haste
		Quickly	
Sire:			Stephanie
Blazing Count			Blenheim
		Mahmoud	
	Obedient		Mah Mahal
			Umidwar
		Uvira	
			Lady Lawless
			Sun Briar
		Pompey	
			Cleopatra
	Ladysman		Polymelian
		Lady Belle	
Dam:			La Grande Armee
Sandy Atlas			Chicle
		Whichone	
	Lotus Flower		Flying Witch
			Waterboy
		Waterblossom	
			Basseting

APPENDIX C
SANDSABLAZE'S MAJOR CAREER HIGHLIGHTS

Year	Event	Placing
1973	AHSA Medal Finals	First
1974	Grand Prix of Ireland	First
1974	Nations Cup (Team), Washington, D.C.	First
1974	Nations Cup (Team), New York	First
1975	Democrat Trophy	First
1975	Cleveland Grand Prix	First
1975	Pan Am Games (Team)	Gold
1975	Nations Cup (Team), New York	First
1975	Nations Cup (Team), Toronto	First
1975	Nations Cup (Team), Washington, D.C.	First
1975	Puissance, Toronto	First (Tie)
1976	Olympic Games (Team)	Fourth
1977	Nations Cup (Team), Washington, D.C.	First
1977	President's Cup	First
1977	Nations Cup (Team), New York	First
1978	Nations Cup (Team), New York	First
1979	Pan Am Games (Team)	Gold
1979	Garden State Grand Prix	First

APPENDIX D
WINNERS OF THE USEF (FORMERLY AHSA) MEDAL FINALS

Year	Winner
1948	Barbara Pease
1949	Nancy Jane Imboden
1950	Ronnie Mutch
1951	Victor Hugo-Vidal
1952	George H. Morris
1953	Cynthia A. Stone
1954	Margaret McGinn
1955	Wilson Dennehy
1956	Michael Page
1957	Michael Del Blaso
1958	Susan White
1959	Wendy Hanson
1960	Mary Mairs
1961	Bernie Traurig
1962	Carol Altmann
1963	Stephanie Steck
1964	James Kohn
1965	Chrystine Jones
1966	Rita Timpanero
1967	Conrad Homfeld
1968	Brooke Hodgson
1969	Fred Bauer

1970	James Hulick
1971	Joy Slater
1972	Katie Monahan
1973	Buddy Brown
1974	Robin Ann Rost
1975	Cynthia Hankins
1976	Frances Steinwedell
1977	Elizabeth Sheehan
1978	Hugh Mutch
1979	Mark Leone
1980	Joan Scharffenberger
1981	Laura Tidball
1982	Sandra Nielsen
1983	Laura O'Connor
1984	Francesca Mazzella
1985	Jenno Topping
1986	Mia Wood
1987	Karen Nielsen
1988	Cheryl Wilson
1989	Ray Texel
1990	Nicole Shahinian
1991	Laura Bowden
1992	Jennifer Clarkson
1993	Melanie Walters
1994	Keri Potter
1995	Meredith Taylor
1996	Hillary Schlusemeyer
1997	Lauren Bass
1998	Kent Farrington
1999	Emily Williams
2000	Sarah Willeman
2001	Randy Sherman
2002	Maggie Jayne
2003	Lauren Van Eldik
2004	Megan Young
2005	Brianne Goutal
2006	Maggie McAlary
2007	Kimberly McCormick
2008	Kels Anabelle Bonham

2009	Jessica Springsteen
2010	Hayley Barnhill
2011	Schafer Raposa
2012	Meg O'Meara
2013	Lillie Keenan

WINNERS OF THE GRAND PRIX OF IRELAND

Year	Winner	Country
1934	Commandant J.G. O'Dwyer	IRL
1935	Oberl Brandt	SUI
1936	Lieutenant de Bartillat	SUI
1937	Miss M. Brown	GBR
1938	Capt F.A. Aherne	IRL
1939	Commandant D.J. Corry	IRL
1940–45	No Show	
1946	Lieutenant Tubridy	IRL
1947	Captain S. Holm	SWE
1948	Miss Iris Kellett	IRL
1949	Miss A.E. Hall	IRL
1950	Mrs. Teeling	IRL
1951	Miss M. McDowell	IRL
1952	Mrs. Teeling	IRL
1953	Captain M.G. Tubridy	IRL
1954	Miss Shirley Thomas	CAN
1955	Lieutenant P.J. Kiernan	IRL
1956	Lieutenant Colonel J. Hume Dudgeon	IRL
1957	Jean d'Orgeix	FRA
1958	George Morris	USA
1959	O. Vanlandeghem	IRL
1960	David Broome	GBR

1961	Tommy Wade	IRL
1962	Captain Piero d'Inzeo	ITA
1963	Tommy Wade	IRL
1964	Miss Kathy Kusner	USA
1965	Miss Kathy Kusner	USA
1966	Hon Diana Conolly-Carew	IRL
1967	David Broome	GBR
1968	David Broome	GBR
1969	Captain R. d'Inzeo	ITA
1970	Harvey Smith	GBR
1971	Graham Fletcher	GBR
1972	Alwin Schockemöhle	GER
1973	Johan Heins	NED
1974	Buddy Brown	USA
1975	Major R d'Inzeo	ITA
1976	Harvey Smith	GBR
1977	David Broome	GBR
1978	Michael Saywell	GBR
1979	David Broome	GBR
1980	Harvey Smith	GBR
1981	David Broome	GBR
1982	Malcolm Pyrah	GBR
1983	Harvey Smith	GBR
1984	Hendrik Snoek	GER
1985	Nick Skelton	GBR
1986	Captain Gerry Mullins	IRL
1987	Paul Darragh	IRL
1988	Nick Skelton	GBR
1989	Nelson Pessoa	BRA
1990	Nick Skelton	GBR
1991	Nick Skelton	GBR
1992	Hauke Luther	GER
1993	Michael Whitaker	GBR
1994	John Whitaker	GBR
1995	Patrice Delaveau	FRA
1996	Eddie Macken	IRL
1997	Robert Smith	GBR
1998	Nick Skelton	GBR
1999	John Whitaker	GBR

2000	Cameron Hanley	IRL
2001	Markus Fuchs	SUI
2002	Marc Houtzager	NED
2003	Wim Schroder	NED
2004	Sheila Burke	USA
2005	Jean Claude van Geenberghe	BEL
2006	Molly Ashe	USA
2007	Comdt Gerry Flynn	IRL
2008	Jessica Kuerten	IRL
2009	Toni Hassman	GER
2010	Mclain Ward	USA
2011	Lauren Hough	USA
2012	Carsten-Otto Nagel	GER
2013	Cian O'Connor	IRL

WINNERS OF THE CLEVELAND GRAND PRIX

Year	Horse	Rider
1965	Tomboy	Mary Chapot
1966	Silver Lining	Carlene Blunt
1967	Gustavus	Rodney Jenkins
1968	Canadian Club	Jim Day
1969	Lights Out	J. Moffat Dunlap
1970	Toy Soldier	Steve Stephens
1971	Grey Carrier	Frank Chapot
1972	Rosie Report	Michael Matz
1973	Springdale	Bernie Traurig
1974	Coming Attraction	Thom Hardy
1975	Sandsablaze	Buddy Brown
1976	Balbuco	Conrad Homfeld
1977	Idle Dice	Rodney Jenkins
1978	The Cardinal	Bernie Traurig
1979	Second Balcony	Rodney Jenkins
1980	Abdullah	Debbie Shaffner
1981	Jet Run	Michael Matz
1982	Noren	Katie Monahan
1983	Jethro	Katie Monahan
1984	Brussels	George Morris
1985	Corsair	Norman Dello Joio
1986	Albany	Debbie Dolan

1987	Gem Twist	Greg Best
1988	Northern Magic	Beezie Patton
1989	Dury Lad	Donald Cheska
1990	Boysie II	James Young
1991	Oxo	Peter Leone
1992	Daydream	Margie Goldstein
1993	Samsung Woodstock	Susie Hutchinson
1994	N/A	N/A
1995	N/A	N/A
1996	Yankee Zulu	Todd Minikus
1997	Hidden Creek's Glory	Margie Goldstein-Engle
1998	Grand Jete	Ellen Talbert
1999	Adam	Margie Goldstein-Engle
2000	Hidden Creek's Laurel	Margie Goldstein-Engle
2001	Sundance Kid	Laura Chapot
2002	Espadon	Candice King
2003	Julius	Margie Engle
2004	Hidden Creek's Wapino	Margie Engle
2005	Hidden Creek's Wapino	Margie Engle
2006	Hidden Creek's Wapino	Margie Engle
2007	Nerina	Kent Farrington
2008	Hidden Creek's Pamina L	Margie Engle
2009	Accordian	Robert Kraut
2010	Indigo	Margie Engle
2011	Toronto	Candice King
2012	Crossfire 10	Federico Sztyrle
2013	Twister	Shawn Casady

RESULTS OF THE 1976 OLYMPIC GAMES–TEAM SHOW JUMPING

Round One

Rank	Team	Faults
1T	France	24.00
1T	West Germany	24.00
3	Canada	28.00
4	Spain	31.00
5	Mexico	31.75
6	Belgium	32.00
7	United States	40.00
8	Great Britain	44.00
9T	Australia	48.00
9T	Italy	48.00
11	Austria	52.00
12	Netherlands	60.00
13	Japan	67.25
14	Argentina	DNF

Round Two

Rank	Team	Faults
1	France	16.00
2	West Germany	20.00

3	United States	24.00
4	Belgium	31.00
5	Great Britain	32.00
6	Canada	36.50
7	Spain	40.00
8	Mexico	44.50

Final Standings

Rank	Team	Medal	Faults
1	France	Gold	40.00
2	West Germany	Silver	44.00
3	Belgium	Bronze	63.00
4	United States		64.00
5	Canada		64.50
6	Spain		71.00
7	Great Britain		76.00
8	Mexico		76.25
9T	Australia		48.00
9T	Italy		48.00
11	Austria		52.00
12	Netherlands		60.00
13	Japan		67.25
AC	Argentina		DNQ

WINNERS OF THE PRESIDENT'S CUP

Year	Winner	Country
1961	Sheriff	Argentina
1962	Unusual	USA
1963	Ilona	Germany
1964	N/A	N/A
1965	San Lucas	USA
1966	Trick Track	USA
1967	Night Spree	USA
1968	Triple Crown	USA
1969	El Ganso	Argentina
1970	Idle Dice	USA
1971	Idle Dice	USA
1972	Scotch Valley	Canada
1973	The Robber	West Germany
1974	Rocket	France
1975	Vicomte Aubiner	West Germany
1976	Number One Spy	USA
1977	Sandsablaze	USA
1978	Texas	Canada
1979	Chase the Clouds	USA
1980	Jet Run	USA
1981	Calypso	USA
1982	Noren	USA

1983	I Love You	USA
1984	Touch of Class	USA
1985	Brussels	USA
1986	The Natural	USA
1987	Special Envoy	USA
1988	Zadok	USA
1989	Everest Oyster	Great Britain
1990	Thrilling	USA
1991	Uncle Sam	USA
1992	Alemao	Canada
1993	Crown Royal Artos	USA
1994	Hauser's Banghi Del Folee	USA
1995	Mistral	Canada
1996	Can Can	USA
1997	Pernod's Roscoe	USA
1998	Crown Royal Legato	USA
1999	Innocence	USA
2000	Glasgow	USA
2001	Nonix LeParc	USA
2002	Conquest II	USA
2003	Picasso 52	USA
2004	Goldika 559	USA
2005	Madison	USA
2006	Exquis Oliver Q	USA
2007	Black Ice	USA
2008	Sapphire	USA
2009	Alaska	USA
2010	Sapphire	USA
2011	Carlo 273	Great Britain
2012	Cylana	USA
2013	Blue Angel	USA

NOTES

1. http://www.spiletta.com/UTHOF/countfleet.html.
2. http://content.time.com/time/magazine/article/0,9171,881867,00.html.
3. http://www.spiletta.com/UTHOF/countfleet.html.
4. *Chronicle of the Horse*, "Horse of a Lifetime: Sandsablaze," August 19, 2013.
5. Ibid.
6. Ibid.
7. *Chronicle of the Horse*, August 19, 2013.
8. *New York Times*, May 26, 1974.
9. William Steinkraus, *The USET Book of Riding* (New York: Simon & Schuster, 1976).
10. *New York Times*, May 1974.
11. *Chronicle of the Horse*, August 19, 2013.
12. http://www.dublinhorseshow.com/index.jsp?p=348&n=432.
13. *Irish Times*, August 12, 1974.
14. *Ann Arbor News*, March 9, 1975.
15. http://www.wihs.org/.
16. *Sports Illustrated*, "A Country Boy Has Them Jumping," November 25, 1974.
17. *New York Times*, November 6, 1974.
18. Ibid.
19 *New York Times*, November 12, 1974.
20. *Cleveland Plain Dealer*, July 24, 1975.
21. Ibid., July 26, 1975.
22. *Cleveland Plain Dealer*, July 27, 1975.

23. *New York Times*, October 31, 1977.
24. Ibid., October 31, 1977.
25. *New York Times*, November 2, 1977.
26. Ibid., November 25, 1977.
27. *Chronicle of the Horse*, "Horse of a Lifetime: Sandsablaze," August 19, 2013.
28. Ibid.
29. *Chronicle of the Horse*, August 1979.

INDEX

T

Tuscaloosa 75, 92, 95, 116

V

Viscount 110, 115

W

Washington International Horse
      Show 55, 91, 92, 115, 123
Wennol Bechan 51
Whitney Stone Trophy 118

ABOUT THE AUTHOR

Kimberly Gatto is an award-winning author specializing in equestrian and sports-related books. Her published works to date include two horse-related titles, four horse racing histories and several athlete biographies. Kim's work has been included in various publications, including the *Blood Horse*, the *Chronicle of the Horse*, the *Equine Journal* and *Chicken Soup for the Horse Lover's Soul*. Kim's book *Belair Stud* recently won a silver medal in the Feathered Quill Book Awards. Kim is an honors graduate of Boston Latin School and Wheaton College in Massachusetts. A lifelong horsewoman, she is the proud owner of a lovely off-the-track Thoroughbred and an adorable Welsh pony.

ABOUT BUDDY BROWN

A living legend in the equine industry, Buddy Brown has represented the United States on many occasions, both at home and abroad. In addition, he is a prominent clinician and a sought-after course designer. At eighteen years of age, Buddy became the youngest rider to win the Grand Prix of Dublin (a record that he holds to this day). His riding career includes team and individual Pan Am medals, a win in the prestigious American Invitational and multiple wins in the International Jumping Derby. Buddy's vigorous course designing schedule takes him to the top shows and circuits in the United States. Buddy and his wife, Vanessa, train horses and riders at their Derby Hill Farm in California.

Visit us at
www.historypress.net
....
This title is also available as an e-book